I am very grateful to Jay Earley for putting my ideas about polarization into writing, which, up until now, have only been conveyed in trainings or workshops. He has added useful case examples and practical steps and, as usual, his writing is very clear. This is a substantial contribution to the literature on Internal Family Systems Therapy.

— Richard Schwartz, PhD, creator of the IFS model,
author of *Internal Family Systems Therapy,*
You are the One You've Been Waiting For

Unresolved internal polarizations can challenge the most experienced therapists. Recognizing and working effectively with internal conflict is crucial to the success of the IFS Model with all clients. This helpful, readable follow-up to Earley's Self-Therapy offers a step-by-step approach and lively examples for navigating this fascinating territory of the human psyche.

— Susan McConnell, Senior Lead Trainer for
the Center for Self Leadership

Polarities abound in our inner systems, and this book fills a gap in the IFS literature. Jay Earley continues to blaze the trail of making Internal Family Systems Therapy accessible to the masses, while still offering useful insights and guidance to practitioners already grounded in the model.

— Bruce Hersey, LCSW, Altoona, PA

Inner conflict seems to be one of our painful, debilitating human burdens. This remarkable book clearly and systematically shows how to approach those intractable inner arguments in such a way that the conflict is actually transformed into unexpected, creative and harmonious ways of expressing our true inner self.

— Persephone Maywald M.A., Psychologist, Adelaide, Australia.

Clear, smart and immediately usable. Every IFS practitioner needs to read this book to deepen their understanding and strengthen their skill.

— Lisa Spiegel, MA, co-director of Soho Parenting

D1572136

Resolving Inner Conflict

Working Through Polarization
Using
Internal Family Systems Therapy

Jay Earley, PhD

Pattern System Books
Larkspur, California

Pattern System Books
140 Marina Vista Ave.
Larkspur, CA 94939
415-924-5256
www.patternsystembooks.com

ISBN-13: 978-0-9843927-6-6
ISBN-10: 0-9843927-6-9
LCCN: 2011945510

Printed in the United States of America

Contents

Acknowledgments

I AM DEEPLY GRATEFUL TO RICHARD SCHWARTZ, PhD, who created the amazing IFS Model, including the powerful approach to resolving polarization described in this book. Susan McConnell and Bruce Hersey provided detailed and very valuable feedback and suggestions for this book. I also received helpful feedback from Kathy Kommit, Elizabeth Galanti, Persephone Maywald, Janina Tiner, and Bonnie Weiss. My thinking about polarization benefited from discussions at the Northern California IFS Community, the Wednesday IFS Class, and the IFS Polarization Telecourse.

Kira Freed did a excellent job of editing and proofreading. Jeannene Chase-Langford produced a fine book cover, and Marny K. Parkin did the interior book design.

Introduction

THIS BOOK IS WRITTEN PRIMARILY FOR INTERNAL FAMILY Systems (IFS) therapists and practitioners. It will also be useful for therapists unfamiliar with IFS since it presents a very effective way of working with internal conflict, which is an important aspect of the human psyche. And if you are a non-therapist who has read my book *Self-Therapy*, this book will expand your understanding of IFS and how to use it to work on yourself. *Self-Therapy* covers the basics of the IFS Model. It's a manual for IFS that can be used by both therapists and laypeople. However, there wasn't space in that book to cover the important IFS work on polarization. This book remedies that situation.

Internal Family Systems Therapy is a cutting-edge psychotherapy approach that has been spreading rapidly around the country and the world over the last decade. It is the signature work of pioneering psychologist Richard Schwartz. IFS is an extremely powerful approach for accessing deep psychological wounds and healing them. It is especially effective with trauma, and there has been increasing interest in IFS among trauma specialists. IFS is also quite effective at helping clients with everyday life issues and with spiritual development.

Schwartz was originally a family systems therapist who started working with his clients' inner worlds and encountered their subpersonalities, which he refers to as *parts*. He realized that his clients' parts were related to each other in systems that were similar to those he recognized in families, hence the name "Internal Family Systems Therapy."[1] IFS is user friendly. It is easy for clients to understand its concepts and natural for most of them to access and relate to their parts.

This book assumes that you already understand the IFS view of the human psyche and the concepts of *part, protector, exile,* and *Self.*[2] I also assume that you understand the IFS process, which includes how work with parts experientially—*unblending* from a part, getting to know a protector, and developing a trusting relationship with it.[3] (See Appendix B for definitions of terms.) If you need to learn these concepts and practices, I recommend that you start with my book *Self-Therapy.* It would also be helpful if you know how to work with and unburden exiles, but you will be able to follow the material in this book without that knowledge.

The approach to working with polarization described in *Resolving Inner Conflict* is the one created by Richard Schwartz and used by experienced IFS therapists. It is an elaboration of the method described by Schwartz in *Internal Family Systems Therapy,* his primary professional book

---

1. For more information on IFS, read *The Internal Family Systems Model* by Richard Schwartz and visit www.selfleadership.org.
2. These concepts are covered in chapters 1 and 2 of *Self-Therapy.*
3. These procedures are covered in chapters 4–8 of *Self-Therapy.*

on IFS.[4] I have emphasized certain aspects of the approach that I favor and have organized it into a series of steps for easy learning.

For years I have been teaching classes on polarization to the general public and also to IFS therapists. This book is based on the material from those classes, and the transcripts are taken from demonstration sessions in those classes.

---

4. p. 120–122.

Chapter 1

Understanding Polarization

H UMAN BEINGS ARE FREQUENTLY IN CONFLICT. WE PRO-crastinate, we are indecisive, we have "mixed feelings," we vacillate, we judge ourselves and then defend against our own judgments. We repress parts of ourselves, which seek to be expressed. If we really listen inside, we can often hear arguments going on between different parts of us. Inner conflict is a major factor in the human psyche.

IFS has ways of understanding inner conflict that illuminate its systems dynamics in a powerful way. It understands three types of inner conflict. First I will discuss *polarization,* since that is the most obvious and extreme form of inner conflict.

When two parts are polarized, it first means that they are opposed to each other. They are attempting to act in contrary ways, such as staying versus going. They form a polarity. However, polarization is more than just polarity. A *polarity* is when two parts (or ideas) are opposites or have opposing tendencies. *Polarization* happens when they go beyond this to actively fighting each other and becoming extreme in reaction to each other. For example, a part that wants to eat a lot would be actively fighting a part that wants to diet. Furthermore, each part is convinced that it must take an extreme stand in order to deal with the destructive actions of the other part.

Imagine two sailors on a sailboat,[5] each of whom is concerned about the boat overturning. One of them is leaning out very far on one side of the boat using a rope to hold himself in that position. He believes that he must lean out that far in order to counteract the other sailor, who is leaning out equally far in the opposite direction. He believes he must be that extreme to keep the boat from capsizing, as does the other sailor. And tragically, they are both right. If either one were to give up his extreme stance and move in to the center of the boat, it would capsize.

This is often the case with polarized parts. They each believe that they must be extreme in their behavior or feelings in order to prevent the other part from doing something very destructive.

Other Types of Inner Conflict in IFS

IFS recognizes a second type of inner conflict between parts. Exiles are child parts that are in pain from events in the past. Protectors attempt to keep exiles out of consciousness so we don't feel their pain. This form of inner conflict is, of course, a major factor in IFS sessions and influences the entire IFS approach.

A third type of inner conflict in IFS comes from a different type of exile. Some exiles are kept out of consciousness not because they are in pain but because they were unacceptable in the milieu in which the person grew up.

---

5. This example comes from Richard Schwartz, the creator of IFS.

Schwartz recognizes this other type of exile but hasn't given it a name. I call them *disowned exiles.*

Let's look at an example. Mary has disowned her assertiveness because it wasn't allowed in her family. When a part is disowned, a conscious part takes its place that represents the opposite, acceptable quality. In Mary's case, this part enacts a meek, placating style of relating. The meek part is a protector that exiles Mary's assertiveness. Mary also has a second protector, an inner critic part that judges her if she shows any signs of personal power. Both of these protectors are involved in a protector-exile type of inner conflict with a disowned exile—Mary's assertive part.

In Mary's family, whenever she stood up for herself, she was hit by her father, which is the way her assertiveness was suppressed. This dynamic produced an exile with a burden of fear, pain, and helplessness as a result of her father's abuse. This is the first kind of exile—the childhood-pain exile. You can see how different this kind of exile is from Mary's assertive part, which is a disowned exile.

As long as an exile (of either kind) simply becomes exiled and disappears from consciousness, these last two kinds of inner conflict don't result in polarization. Or you could say that they result in *one-sided polarization,* in which one part is fighting and the other is not. This is often the case. However, if the exile actively fights to be felt and heard or even to influence the person's behavior, this results in full-blown polarization. For example, when Mary began to re-own her assertiveness through therapy, her inner critic part became threatened and reacted strongly, trying to crush her power. But now this wasn't easy to do, so the two parts actively battled each other for supremacy.

To summarize, there are three kinds of inner conflict in IFS:

1. Polarization

2. The protector-exile relationship with an ordinary childhood-pain exile

3. The protector-exile relationship with a disowned exile.

Inner Conflict in Other Forms of Therapy

The psychodynamic therapies have a major focus on inner conflicts between the forces of the unconscious and the ego and superego. Unconscious forces include primitive instincts and painful or traumatic memories, all of which are actively repressed. The ego and superego, which are the forces of repression, attempt to keep the unconscious locked away. This type of inner conflict shows up in IFS as the second kind of inner conflict mention above—that between protectors and childhood-pain exiles. Psychodynamic theory doesn't seem to recognize polarization, which often involves two parts that are both conscious.

Jung introduced the idea of the shadow, which is that aspect of the unconscious that contains parts that have been disowned because they were unacceptable to the person's family or culture. Voice Dialogue is a method of working with subpersonalities that is based on Jungian ideas, so its understanding of inner conflict is based on the *shadow*. Voice Dialogue emphasizes the conflict between disowned selves (shadow) and primary selves, which are consciously owned aspects of oneself. In IFS, this corresponds to the third kind of inner conflict—between protectors and disowned exiles.

Gestalt Therapy has a method for working with parts that are in conflict—the famous "empty chair" technique, which doesn't include a theoretical understanding of inner conflict. We will compare the Gestalt technique to IFS later in this book.

An Example of Polarization

Bill is working on a big, new marketing project. He works long hours every day and has very little time for his wife and young son. When friends ask why he works so hard or his wife asks why she never sees him, he says, "I want to get ahead. I want to get a quick promotion and become highly successful." However, when looked at objectively, working 50 hours a week would be enough in Bill's company for him to do quite well, but he regularly puts in 60–70 hours and often goes back to work on the weekends. Few people at his firm put in this many hours, even those who are successfully moving up the ladder.

Bill sometimes skips meals. He occasionally works late into the night, even when he has no deadline coming up. He is often so tired the next day that the quality of his work suffers. A Striving Part is driving Bill to work this hard because it is irrationally afraid of failure. It feels it must do everything possible to make sure Bill is a huge success because it is so afraid of any hint of failure.

Bill has a second part that plays a major role in his psychological dynamics around work. When Bill was in the early years of high school, he wasn't a high achiever—quite the opposite. He spent his time having fun rather than doing his homework. He watched a lot of TV. He hung out with friends. He did just about anything except his schoolwork. When he had an important assignment he would procrastinate and then end up doing a rush job that got a poor grade. Sometimes he didn't do his homework at all.

This behavior came from a Procrastinator Part of Bill. This part wanted to avoid doing anything that would be graded or evaluated. It was afraid of failure, and it dealt with this fear by avoiding projects that could involve failure—virtually all school and work projects. This fear was unconscious. If you had asked Bill why he wasn't doing his homework, he would have said he didn't feel like it.

This strategy was doomed, of course. By avoiding projects, Bill ended up feeling like a failure—the very feeling that his Procrastinator was trying to avoid. However, this kind of dynamic is common. Very often our parts cause us to act in ways that go against our best interests, and even go against the protective intent of the part, resulting in exactly what the part is trying to prevent.

Each of Bill's two parts has its own protective reasons for performing its role. In fact, they are both trying to help Bill avoid failure—they just use opposing strategies. The Striver wants to ensure that Bill is a fabulous success, and the Procrastinator wants to avoid trying and failing. Furthermore, each part feels that it must be extreme in order to battle the excesses of the other part.

The Striver says, "I know that Bill has a tendency to be lazy, so I must push him to work very hard in order to combat this tendency. I'm afraid that if I let up even a little, Bill will turn into a bum like he was in high school." The

Procrastinator, on the other hand, says, "I hate the way the Striver acts like a constant taskmaster. I must try my best to get out from under its thumb so Bill can relax and enjoy himself. I'm afraid that if I let go, the Striver will turn Bill's life into a nightmare of constant work." Both parts are trying to protect Bill from failure and from each other.

Aspects of Polarization

Polarization is often about a specific action or decision, such as the amount of time that Bill should spend working. Two parts are at odds over how a client should act. Neither is willing to release *its* extreme role unless the other part has also released its extreme role. Each fears that if it lets go, the other part will take over and cause serious problems. Therefore, you have to work with them both to make it possible for them to shift.

Polarization usually happens between two protectors. In addition to their conflict with each other, each of them is also protecting an exile. They are sometimes polarized about the best way to protect the same exile. In the example with Bill, both the Striver and the Procrastinator were trying to protect an exile who felt like a failure. At other times, each polarized part may be protecting a different exile.

Sometimes the tension and drama of the interaction of polarized parts is in itself a form of protection because it distracts the client from the exile they are protecting. The two apparent archrivals are actually allies in this endeavor.

Sometimes one of two polarized parts will take over for a while, and the other part will be strong-armed into submission or will give up. This can happen for a few hours or days, or sometimes years. Then a switch may occur, and the other part will take over.

When a person has underlying trauma, his or her protectors become more extreme and dysfunctional because of an urgent need to protect the person from reexperiencing the trauma. When one protector becomes extreme and its actions produce hurt and difficulty in the person's life, this triggers other protectors that try to mitigate this trouble. These other protectors often become extreme themselves in an attempt to battle the first ones. They may become harsh inner critics, angrily judging other protectors or exiles. Or they may become rigid and extreme in other ways. In any case, they become polarized with the protectors they are fighting. Because of this, traumatized inner systems tend to have a great deal of extreme polarization.

The Positive Aspects of Polarized Parts

Even though polarized parts are usually extreme, oftentimes they each hold an energy or quality that is important to the client. For example, Bill's Striver held the energy of good work and accomplishment, and his Procrastinator held the energy of relaxation and enjoyment. One common kind of polarization is between the quality of interpersonal connection and the quality of self-assertion, both of which are valuable. Another widespread polarization is between safety/order and autonomy/freedom.

In these situations, you don't want to erase or diminish the positive energy of either polarized part. You want to help the client have access to this energy in a non-extreme, cooperative form.

In resolving polarization, you aren't looking to find a bland compromise between the parts or a negotiated settlement that is purely intellectual. The goal is to have the client's parts appreciate each other's strengths and good intentions, work through their extreme protective roles, and learn to cooperate. This gives the client much greater access to his or her creativity and power and makes it possible for the client to come up with innovative solutions to conflicts that are likely to be satisfying to both parts. A dynamic, transformative process results when the Self can hold space for two polarized parts to work together.

Chapter 2

Recognizing Polarization

THIS BOOK PRESENTS A STEP-BY-STEP PROCEDURE FOR working with polarization. Step 1 involves recognizing when a client is dealing with polarized parts in an IFS session. Here are some tips on how to do this:

Trailheads. When a client is exploring a *trailhead* (a troublesome situation that can lead to growth), you may realize that he or she has opposing or conflicting responses to the situation. For example, Jane had fears about visiting her family because they tend to be so angry and shaming. When she explored her fears, she found that a part of her really didn't want her to go, and a polarized part felt she should. There was also a third part that missed her family since she hadn't seen them for a long time. She had two parts on one side of the polarization and one on the other. This is a common situation.

Decisions. When a client is having trouble making a decision, it almost always involves polarized parts—one that wants to make the decision one way, and one that wants the opposite. In fact, the reason that the client is having trouble deciding is because of the polarized parts. There is often more than one part on each side of this kind of polarization.

Protector Fears. One of the common questions IFS therapists encourage our clients to ask a protector is, "What are you afraid would happen if you didn't perform your role?" When the protector says, "I'm afraid you'll feel shame or be terrified" or some other painful emotion, this usually points to the exile it is protecting, an exile who is feeling that painful emotion. If the protector says, "I'm afraid of someone hurting you" (or controlling you or judging you or harming you in some other way), this also involves an exile, one who was harmed in that way.

However, if the protector says, "I'm afraid you will get really angry" or go on a binge or engage in some other dangerous activity, this usually indicates that the protector is afraid of a polarized part—the part that might engage in that activity. For example, Bill asked his Inner Critic protector, "What are you afraid would happen if you didn't judge me and shame me around my work habits?" The Critic said, "I'm afraid you'll procrastinate and not get much work done." This response indicated that Bill's Critic was afraid of a Procrastinator part that it was polarized with.

Concerned Parts and Polarization

Suppose a client is attempting to get to know a protector and you ask her, "How do you feel toward that part?" She says, "I'm really angry at it, and I'd like to get rid of it." This is coming from another part of her that is interfering with her being in Self—what I call a *concerned part*. This concerned part is sometimes polarized with the protector. For a polarization to exist, both parts must be actively opposing each other. The concerned part is always against

the target part; it is concerned about the target part causing problems. However, the target part may or may not
be fighting back. If it isn't, I call the dynamic a *one-sided
polarization*.

For example, Sarah sometimes gets enraged at her husband, which causes problems in her marriage. This emotion comes from her Angry Part. A different part of Sarah
doesn't like her anger. Let's call this part of Sarah the
Anger Critic. If the Anger Critic is actively trying to stop
Sarah from flying off the handle with her husband, and
the Angry Part is fighting to express anger, this is clearly
a polarization. However, suppose the Angry Critic just
judges the Angry Part; it doesn't really try to stop the anger,
and the Angry Part isn't even aware of it. In that case, it
would be a one-sided polarization, not true polarization.

For there to be true polarization, the parts must be fighting each other. However, this doesn't necessarily mean
that they are talking directly with each other or even
that they are aware of each other as parts. Two parts can
be fighting over how a client will behave without being
in conversation with each other. For example, suppose
Sarah's Anger Critic really tries to stop her from getting
angry. It says, "Don't blow up at him again. Your anger
is ruining your marriage. Just keep it cool this time." The
Anger Critic isn't necessarily aware that there is a *part* of
Sarah that feels angry. And her Angry Part may just be
trying to express its anger against this resistance. The two
parts may not actually be arguing with each other directly,
yet they are still polarized.

In fact, even a hidden, unconscious part can be polarized as long as it is actively engaged in fighting a conscious

part. This dynamic still constitutes a polarization because the two are in conflict. If the hidden part just gives in and allows itself to be pushed aside, this situation isn't a polarization.

Polarity vs. Polarization

Jean has a part that is kind, compassionate, and connecting. This part loves to care for people and be close to them. It tends to become activated when she is with her family or friends. She has another part that is competitive and judgmental. It tries to triumph over others and is often harsh and critical. This part tends to be activated when she is at work. These parts form a *polarity* because they are opposites of each other. However, they don't really fight each other because they tend to come out in different situations. When one part is activated, the other is quiet, and vice versa. Therefore, they aren't polarized.

Sam has a shy part that avoids being the center of attention in any group situation because it is afraid of being judged or ridiculed. He has another part that would love to be the center of attention and be recognized and applauded. However, this part is deeply buried and never takes action in Sam's world. It doesn't even particularly try to come forward because of Sam's fear. These parts also form a polarity because they are opposites, but they aren't polarized because they don't have conflicts with each other. The shy part is always in charge.

Eleanor has a perfectionist part that makes her overwork. As a result, she becomes exhausted. She has another part that feels exhausted and wishes she weren't working so hard. These parts are opposites—a polarity. However, her exhausted part doesn't attempt to stop the overwork—it just feels wiped out and unhappy, so this is not a polarization. If the exhausted part tried to get Eleanor to let up, or if it increased the exhaustion as a way of fighting against the overwork, the dynamic would constitute a polarization.

Manager/Firefighter Polarization

Managers and firefighters are the two types of protectors in IFS, and they are frequently polarized. (If you are unfamiliar with these terms, see Appendix D.)

Managers and *firefighters* are often polarized with each other. Most firefighters tend to be oriented toward excitement and intensity, fun and thrills. Most managers tend to be oriented toward control and order, especially if they are trying to stop the destructive activity of firefighters. In fact, as a result of successful IFS work, some clients will experience a decrease in the extreme feelings that come from firefighters and will begin to feel that their lives have become boring. This difference in orientation between managers and firefighters lends itself toward polarization.

However, there is a bigger reason that managers and firefighters become polarized. Since firefighter activity is often dangerous and self-destructive, managers that are very judgmental of firefighters come forward and try to limit their behavior. In fact, for every harmful firefighter, there will almost always be at least one manager that is polarized with it and is trying to stop it from causing problems in the client's life.

When a manager doesn't succeed in stopping the firefighter, it often becomes harshly judgmental toward the client for engaging in the firefighter activity. It shames the client in an attempt to prevent the firefighter from acting out again.

When a client's life is being ruined by a firefighter, it is easy to think that you only need to work with this part and get it to change its behavior. However, because of the presence of polarization, it usually isn't enough to just work with the destructive firefighter. You must also engage with the controlling manager and work on the polarization directly, as this book shows how to do.

Protector/Exile Polarization

It is also possible for a polarization to exist between a protector (which could be either a manager or a firefighter) and an exile. This happens when the exile blends with the client and attempts to take action in real-life situations. Some exiles are hidden from consciousness and are only accessed during IFS sessions. These exiles usually don't create polarizations. However, certain exiles tend to actually take over at times and influence the way a person behaves.

For example, Betty had a Needy Part (exile) that often took over when she was in a love relationship and made her dependent on her partner. Her Needy Part was polarized with a Distancing Part (protector) that tried to keep her out of relationships so she wouldn't become so dependent. This protector was trying to protect the Needy Part from being in pain by keeping Betty out of relationships. It was also polarized with the Needy Part because that exile longed to be in an intimate relationship, and the protector was trying to prevent her from having one.

There is also another way in which an exile can be polarized with a protector. Sometimes an exile will actively push toward expressing its painful emotions consciously. It wants to be known and tries to bring its pain to the client's attention. If this push is opposed by a protector that is trying to keep the pain hidden, these parts are polarized. This dynamic is particularly acute with trauma, where a polarization can exist between a traumatized exile that gets hyperaroused at times and a dissociating or numbing protector that attempts to block this from occurring.

Other Examples of Polarization

Here are some additional examples of polarization:

Clients who have a harsh Inner Critic part often have another part, which I call the Inner Defender, that tries to argue with the Critic to prove it wrong. If the Critic says that a client is stupid, the Inner Defender tries to show how intelligent he is. If the Critic says that a woman is a loser with men, the Defender points out how many men are attracted to her. Very often the two parts battle it out, and the Critic frequently wins.

A client may have a polarization between a part that is aggressive in interpersonal conflicts and one that wants to avoid them. Elise has a protector that gets very angry when conflicts come up in her marriage. She has another part that tries to prevent conflict in order to avoid these angry outbursts. This part leaves the room or becomes placating when a conflict starts. Since the angry part is often eager to engage in an argument, these parts become polarized about how to deal with interpersonal difficulties.

There is sometimes a polarization between the part of a client that brings the client into therapy because it wants help and a part that is afraid of potential pain during the therapy process or a part that resists change. One part will block or sabotage the therapy process, while the other part keeps bringing the client to sessions and asking for help. This dynamic can be frustrating for the therapist until you recognize this polarization and work with it.

Deciding Whether to Focus on the Polarization

Just because you recognize a polarization doesn't mean that you should always deal with it directly. Sometimes you can just work with one of the polarized parts in the ordinary IFS way. You focus on one of the parts—a protector. The client gets to know it and develops a trusting relationship with it.[6] Then you obtain its permission to work with the exile it is protecting and go through the steps of healing and unburdening that exile.[7] As a result, the protector may be ready to let go of its extreme role despite the polarization. This may allow the other polarized part to relax, too. In this way, the polarization may be resolved without the need to work with it directly. This approach can be sufficient if the polarization isn't particularly intense.

However, in many cases, this is not enough, and you need to work directly on the polarization. How do you decide if this is necessary? One way is to simply start

---

6. For a detailed explanation of this process, see chapters 4–8 of *Self-Therapy.*

7. For a detailed explanation of this process, see chapters 10–14 of *Self-Therapy.*

working with one of the polarized parts and see how far you get. If you run into problems—for example, if the other part keeps jumping in and attacking the part you are focused on—this may indicate that you need to focus on the polarization.

Another possibility: You might follow through completely with one part and unburden its exile, but you realize, after awhile, that the client's behavior isn't changing. This probably means that you must also work on the polarization directly.

If you sense that a lot of energy is tied up in the fight between the polarized parts, it makes sense to focus on the polarization directly rather than trying to work with one part. For example, when you ask the target part what it is afraid would happen if it didn't perform its role, if its answer points to the polarized part, it is probably more concerned with that part than with the exile.

There is another common reason it can be useful to focus on a polarization. Suppose the client is so blended with a protector that she doesn't realize that it is causing problems in her life. The client brought up the part to work on when she wasn't so blended, but now the part has taken over, and she simply repeats the part's rationalization for its role. If you can't get the client to unblend, you won't be able to investigate the problematic aspects of the part's role since the client (as the part) doesn't think there are any.

However, you will often hear from a part that is polarized with the target part. If you focus on that polarization, this polarized part will have its say, and you can work on the conflict between them. This will clearly bring to light the problems with the original protector, which the client couldn't see due to being blended with it.

For example, Page has a part that is a caretaker. She goes out of her way to focus on other people's needs to make sure they aren't uncomfortable and feel safe. She does this to the exclusion of being aware of her own needs. Page brings this up in a session because she realizes it is causing problems in her life. But as she is getting to know the Caretaker Part, it subtly blends with her, so when she asks what it is trying to accomplish, it says it cares about people and naturally wants them to be happy. At this point, Page can't see any problems with the Caretaker because it has taken her over. If you tried to point out her problems with caretaking, you would likely get resistance from that part.

However, as the Caretaker is talking, Page hears from another part that is sick and tired of taking care of all these ungrateful people at the expense of her own needs. This part is polarized with the Caretaker. By focusing on the polarization and giving this part a voice, the problems with the Caretaker will become apparent without your having to bring them up. You can remain a neutral party who isn't taking sides.

Polarization Procedure

The following is a sequence of steps for working with polarization, which will be covered in the rest of this book. These steps are an elaboration of the procedure developed by Richard Schwartz, the founder of IFS. It is described in brief in his book *Internal Family Systems Therapy.*[8]

---

8. p. 120–122.

1. Recognize and identify the polarized parts.

2. Facilitate the client in unblending from each part in order to access Self.

   a. Have the client hold each part in consciousness at the same time.

   b. Ask each part to step aside so the client can get to know the other part.

   c. Have the client reassure each part that he or she will get to know it, too, and won't let the other part take over.

3. Facilitate the client in getting to know each part's role, positive intent, and conflict with the other part.

   a. Unblend from any concerned parts.

   b. Find out what the part is trying to do for the client.

   c. Find out how the part feels toward the polarized part and how it counters it.

   d. Develop a trusting relationship between the client's Self and each part.

4. Decide whether to work with an exile or engage in a depolarization dialogue.

5. Have the client get permission from each part to have a depolarization dialogue with the other part under the guidance of Self.

   a. Reassure each part that Self won't allow the other part to take over or attack.

6. Facilitate the beginning of the depolarization dialogue.

    a. Decide whether to do it internally or externally.

    b. Have each part state its position and respond to the other part.

    c. Continue the process until the positions and conflict are clear.

7. Facilitate true dialogue and resolution.

    a. Each part reveals the exile it is protecting.

    b. Each part listens to the other's concerns and fears, and responds accordingly.

    c. Either a part, the Self, or the therapist suggests a resolution.

    d. Each part considers the potential resolution and brings up concerns and suggestions for improving it.

    e. The parts negotiate with each other and Self in order to come to a resolution they can both agree to.

Chapter 3

Unblending from Polarized Parts

S TEP 2 IN WORKING WITH POLARIZATION IS TO MAKE SURE the client is not blended with either polarized part so he or she can connect with each part from Self.[9] Clients often start out in a state in which they are blended with both parts and are feeling torn inside. Or they bounce back and forth between the two parts, first being blended with one and then the other part. For example, a client who is polarized around eating will vacillate between being blended with a ravenous part and with a part that is trying to adhere to a strict diet.

Here is one simple way to facilitate unblending from both parts. Ask the client to hold both polarized parts in his or her awareness at the same time. For example, ask the client to imagine a room in which he or she invites each part to sit down in a separate chair, or encourage the client to hold one part in each hand or feel each part in his or her body. This tends to unblend[10] the client from both

---

9. For a definition of Self and other technical terms, see Appendix B.

10. For an explanation of unblending from protectors, see chapter 5 of *Self-Therapy*.

parts. It is helpful to have the client become grounded in his or her body before facilitating this unblending.

However, some clients don't have an easy time being aware of both parts, so here is a surer method. Have the client negotiate with each part (one at a time) to unblend so he or she can get to know the other part. Let's call them Part A and Part B. The client, Terri, asks Part B to step aside temporarily and let her get to know Part A. She reassures Part B that she won't let Part A take over and do destructive things, and that she will return to Part B and get to know it after she has worked with Part A. Hopefully this is enough to convince Part B to step aside. Then Terri also asks Part A to separate from her so she can get to know it, as is standard in IFS with a protector.

If the client has difficulty getting into Self in order to conduct his negotiation, you as the therapist may have to facilitate the process by talking directly to each part. This application of the IFS technique is called *direct access.*

Here is an example of this unblending process. Dan tends to drink too much. This behavior comes from a firefighter that he calls the Drinker. He also has a Drink Controller part, which is a manager that tries to keep him from drinking too much. Whenever Dan begins to drink, this manager tries to get him to limit himself to a couple of drinks. Sometimes it succeeds, and at other times the Drinker wins and Dan gets really drunk. When this happens, the next day the Drink Controller castigates him, telling him that he is an alcoholic loser. This example shows a classic type of polarization.

When Dan started working with these two polarized parts, he decided to start by getting to know the Drinker.

However, the Drink Controller immediately took over, making Dan feel judgmental and disgusted with the Drinker. Dan was clearly not in Self; he was blended with the Drink Controller, so he wasn't be able to work successfully with the Drinker. He asked the Controller to step aside so he could get to know the Drinker part from an open place. The Drink Controller said, "No way! That part just causes problems in your life. You should get rid of it—not talk to it."

Dan's therapist helped him know how to respond. He coached Dan in saying to the Drink Controller, "You can't get rid of parts. The only way to change destructive behavior is to get to know the part from an accepting place and discover what it is trying to do for me. All parts have a positive intent, so if you let me, I could make a connection with the Drinker and help to transform it. You know, your strategy hasn't been working very well, so how about trying something new?"

Once Dan had explained these things, his therapist tried to facilitate an unblending. He had Dan say, "Would you be willing to separate from me so I can work with the Drinker in this way?" The Drink Controller was willing to see if this would work, since it had to admit that its strategy hadn't been working.

Dan then proceeded to get to know the Drinker. He wasn't blended with it at the time because there wasn't any current issue that was bringing up exile pain, so the Drinker wasn't activated.

While a client is getting to know Part A, Part B may jump in and disrupt the process if it feels threatened. When this happens, the client needs to negotiate again with Part B and see if it will trust the client enough to let the session continue. If not, the client may have to work with Part B first.

For example, while Dan was working with the Drinker, it told him how it drank to prevent him from feeling rejected. The Drink Controller jumped in and said, "That's a really stupid approach. It doesn't help at all. It just makes matters worse." When the therapist suggested that Dan ask the Drink Controller to step aside, it was so disgusted with the Drinker that it wasn't willing to. So Dan switched his attention to the Drink Controller and got to know it first.

Of course, in order to do that, he needed to be separate from the Drinker. In this case, that wasn't a problem since the Drinker wasn't blended with him, so he was able to go ahead and work with the Drink Controller first. Then, after he had connected with it, the Drink Controller had no trouble allowing him to work with the Drinker because it now trusted him.

Identifying with One Side of a Polarization

A different blended situation sometimes arises with polarization. A client may be so identified (blended) with one part of a polarization that he or she doesn't recognize the polarization at all. The client just thinks that he or she is trying to work with a difficult protector without realizing that he or she has become blended with a polarized part.

For example, suppose Dan started out just thinking that he had to get the Drinker to stop bingeing. He assumed he was in Self and was dealing with a destructive part. In fact, he was very worried about the damage that the

Drinker was causing in his life, so it wasn't surprising that he might not be very open to it. Dan was actually blended with the Drink Controller, but he couldn't observe himself, so he couldn't see that he wasn't actually in Self. In this case, it is up to you, the therapist, to recognize that the client isn't in Self and to point out the polarization so it can be worked on directly.

A related danger is that you might be blended with a part of you that is also taking sides in the polarization—a part that feels critical of one of the client's parts or wants to get rid of it. This part of the client may be causing him a lot of problems or putting him in danger, so it isn't surprising that you might feel negatively toward it. Often you and the client are both taking sides in a polarization without realizing it. Clearly your first priority is to recognize this situation in yourself and to unblend from your critical part and return to Self. Then you will be able to see that the client is also blended and taking sides, so you can help him to return to Self.

Chapter 4

Getting to Know a Polarized Part

O NCE THE CLIENT HAS UNBLENDED FROM EACH POLAR-
ized part, you can proceed to Step 3, getting to
know each polarized part and developing a trusting relationship with it.

Follow the usual procedure that you already know for
getting to know a protector.[11] Have the client find out the
part's role in his psyche and its positive intent for him.
Two important questions to ask protectors are: What are
you trying to accomplish by performing the role? What are
you afraid would happen if you didn't perform your role?

This process will lead toward an understanding of
what the protector is trying to protect the client from. It
is especially important to understand the positive intent
of a polarized part because its behavior can sometimes be
quite extreme and destructive, or at least look that way
to the part it is polarized with. Finding out its positive
intent goes a long way toward helping the other part not
to vilify it so much.

For example, Dan discovers that his Drinker is trying
to protect a young exile who was deeply wounded by his

---

11. For a detailed explanation of this process, see chapter 7 of
Self-Therapy.

mother's rejection. The Drinker feels that this pain is intolerable and must be suppressed at all costs. Once Dan (and the Drink Controller) became aware of the pain this exile was carrying, they were more sympathetic to the extremes of the Drinker. This doesn't mean they felt it was OK to abuse alcohol; it just means that they had more understanding of the Drinker's dilemma.

The Drink Controller was trying to protect a number of exiles who were triggered by the consequences of Dan's drinking. One exile felt ashamed when Dan got drunk and out of control. Another exile was afraid of abandonment since Dan's marriage was in trouble because of his drinking.

While the client is getting to know each part, have him ask how it feels toward the part it is polarized with and what it does to counter the other part's feelings or actions. This gives both you and the client a clearer sense of the polarization dynamics.

For example, the Drink Controller hates the Drinker and is ashamed of it and its behavior. The Drink Controller tries to keep Dan from drinking at all, or at least to limit his drinking. When this fails, it shames the Drinker to try to keep it from repeating this behavior in the future. Of course, this shaming just makes Dan feel worse about himself, and, in fact, it backfires by making the Drinker more likely to go on a bender in the future in order to protect the ashamed exile.

The Drinker tries to counter the Drink Controller's rigidity about alcohol. It feels oppressed and shamed by the Drink Controller and hates it. The Drinker's strategy is to make Dan unconscious of consequences (not be aware of the Drink Controller) so he can drink as much as he wants. You can see that each part becomes more extreme in trying to counter the other.

Developing a Trusting Relationship with a Polarized Part

Have clients let each part know that they understand why it performs its role and appreciate its efforts on their behalf. It is especially important for the client to create a trusting relationship with each polarized part. He will have to be the mediator (under your guidance) between these parts when they dialogue with each other. Since the parts usually start out hating each other, dialogue can be difficult to achieve. They will only allow a client to do this if they really trust him or her. Otherwise, one part may start to act out as soon as the opposing part begins to speak.

Let's look at an example with Dan and his parts. Dan said to the Drink Controller, "I appreciate your efforts to limit my drinking. I understand the pain and difficulties that the drinking is causing, and I want to stop, too." This helped the Drink Controller feel that Dan was on his side, so it wasn't as outraged when Dan also made a connection with the Drinker.

When Dan got to know the Drinker, he said, "I appreciate your efforts to protect the young child part who was so wounded by my mother. I know you go to extremes with your drinking, but I understand that you do it because you think I couldn't tolerate feeling that pain." This helped the Drinker feel connected to Dan and trust him.

Once the client has expressed appreciation to one of the polarized parts, check to see if the part is able to take in this appreciation.[12] If the part doesn't trust the client, check to make sure that the client is still in Self and help him or her to get there, if necessary. Or if the part has trust issues because of the client's history, work on this directly.

Dealing with Trust Issues

One part may not trust the client because it believes that the client has been favoring the part it is polarized with. If this is true, have the client admit it and explain, "I don't want to do that anymore. That's why I want to get to know you both and resolve the polarization." If that isn't true, help the client to explain what his or her attitude is toward each polarized part so that the mistrustful part can realize that the client really is in Self and is therefore open and interested in both parts.

For example, suppose that Dan's Drink Controller didn't trust him. It might say, "You've been allowing all this binge drinking to go on. How do you expect me to trust that you appreciate my efforts to stop this craziness? It seems as if you really favor the Drinker." Dan could respond, from Self, "You're right. I *have* allowed way too much drinking to happen. And I don't feel good about that, either. But it hasn't been because I support that kind of behavior. It's because I haven't been in Self. The Drinker just took over and did the drinking. I'm trying to stop that now by having this dialogue between you and the Drinker." This explanation should help the Drink Controller to trust Dan.

_____

12. For a detailed explanation of this process, see chapter 8 of *Self-Therapy.*

As each part develops a trusting relationship with Self, the polarization may decrease as a result of this step alone. Protectors start out not realizing that the Self exists or that it is a source of understanding, compassion, and strength. The beauty of IFS is that when our parts recognize the Self and connect with it, they tend to become more collaborative and have more Self-energy inside themselves.

Chapter 5

Transcript of
Getting to Know Polarized Parts

T HE FOLLOWING IS THE FIRST SEGMENT OF A TRANSCRIPT
of a session with a participant in one of my polarization
classes. It shows Steps 2 and 3 of the process—unblending from both polarized parts, getting to know them, and
developing a trusting relationship with each of them.

Jay: Anne, tell me about the polarized parts that you
want to work with.

Anne: Well, there's a part that feels strongly like it
wants to make a contribution. It wants me to make
a contribution in the world—in a big way, like for
me to lead workshops, write books, or be out there
in some big way, be helping humanity to evolve in
some way.

Then I have this other part that's really polarized
with it, that just doesn't want to have anything to do
with people. It doesn't want to be out there; it just
wants to be in my apartment, alone with nature. That
part thinks the other part has been brainwashed by
my family, because I come from a family of political
activists. It thinks the desire to make some kind of
difference comes from conditioning. The part that

35

wants to make a difference thinks the other part is some kind of pathology from my childhood.

J: So they each have pretty strong judgments about the other one.

Notice that each part feels negatively toward the other.

A: Yeah, they do.

J: OK. Just take a moment right now, and check and see if it feels like you're blended with either of those parts right now.

In order to successfully do polarization work, the client must not be blended with either part so she can get to know them from Self.

A: It feels like I'm a little bit blended with the part that wants to stay away from people—just because I had weird interactions with some people this morning.

J: OK.

A: I feel like people are a pain in the butt, you know?

J: OK, so ask that part if it would be willing to separate from you so that you can get to know it and help it—just in this session, not necessarily at other times.

A: Yeah, it's actually pretty happy to, and it's pretty interested in this process.

J: OK.

A: It's happy to cooperate.

J: All right, good, thank it for that. So I'd like to have you get to know each of these parts in turn. Do you have any sense of which part you'd like to start with?

A: The part that just separated, the Stay Away Part, says I should start with the other part, the Life Purpose Part. It says to go ahead and let the other one speak first. It's being very cooperative. And the Life Purpose Part really wants to speak.

J: OK, let's go with that. Take a second to access the Life Purpose Part, if you haven't already, and let me know when you feel it in your body or have an image of it.

A: OK, I felt this kind of upswelling of energy around my heart—like this part is here now, and I'm in touch with it.

J: And how are you feeling toward that part right now?

A: I'm feeling some affection for it. I guess you could say that I'm feeling fond of it.

This is the check to see if Anne is in Self with respect to the Life Purpose Part. She needs to not only be unblended from it but also interested in getting to know it from an open place. It seems that she is.

J: So invite the part to tell you what its role is or what it wants for you.

A: It wants me to be out there, to be making a contribution of some sort. I have a lot of knowledge that could be useful to some people and ways of accessing inner life that a lot of people don't know about. It thinks I have a lot to contribute, and it feels passionate about my doing that.

J: OK, ask the part what it hopes to get or accomplish by having you do that.

A: Well, you know something really interesting flashed through my mind when you asked me that question. This part thinks I'm going to prove myself worthy in some way. That's really new information for me. That part thinks this is a way to prove myself worthy to other people.

J: Ask the part what that would do for you if you proved yourself worthy.

A: This is so funny. It's like there's some little wounded, humiliated exile that would be vindicated.

J: OK. There's an exile inside that's feeling humiliated and wounded, and the Life Purpose Part wants to protect it by having you be out there making a contribution and having people recognize your worth. Is that right?

A: Yeah, and this part sees that when I was little, people made fun of me. They thought I was weird and criticized me for being too sensitive, and the exile got wounded by this. Being sensitive is a gift—it's not a liability at all. So somehow this protector wants to kind of turn things around for the exile. It wants to have the exile experience that its sensitivity is what is powerful.

Some of its motivation feels like a natural expression of my gifts, but there's also this edge to it. It wants to show everybody that they were wrong about me when they devalued my sensitivity.

J: Right, so there are two aspects of this part's motivation. One is just a natural desire to manifest your gifts and live your life's purpose, and the other is to protect the exile.

A: Yeah.

As is often the case, one aspect of the Life Purpose Part's motivation is healthy, and one is "extreme." The desire to express her gifts and make a difference in the world is healthy. The desire to prove that her sensitivity is valuable rather than bad is more extreme (dysfunctional) because it comes from a need to protect that exile in her who was humiliated when she was a child. This is the protective side of the Life Purpose Part.

J: See if there's anything else this protector wants you to know about itself.

A: No, that's really what it wanted to say.

J: And are you feeling appreciative of this part, of what it's trying to do for you?

A: Oh, yeah—totally.

J: Yeah, I figured you were. So let the part know that. It may already have known that, but just in case it didn't, let the part know of your appreciation for it.

A: OK.

J: And how is it responding to you?

A: It likes feeling acknowledged. It feels … just calm, like it's been seen, and that feels good.

Anne has not only discovered the Life Purpose Part's role, she has also made a nice connection with it by expressing her appreciation. This will help when the two parts dialogue with each other.

J: Good. Now ask the part how it feels toward this other part, the Stay Away Part.

A: It feels really angry toward that part. It feels like that part is trying to sabotage it all the time.

J: All right. So let's just check and see if it's OK with the Life Purpose Part for you to now get to know the Stay Away Part.

A: It wants some reassurance that I'm not going to just let the other part run things.

J: Yeah, so reassure it that you are only going to get to know the Stay Away Part, and you won't let it take over.

A: Yeah. Now it is willing.

At first, the Life Purpose Part was hesitant to allow Anne to get to know the other part for fear that it would take over and keep her away from people. However, she reassured it that she wouldn't let that happen, and then it granted permission.

J: So focus on the other part.

A: OK.

J: Do you have an image or a body sense of the other part?

A: It's like a bighorn sheep with giant horns, and it bucks everything to keep it away. It's very protective, and it likes to run into things and smash them to make them go away. This Sheep Part isn't very tactful.

As she has gotten to know this part better, its name has changed. This is fairly common.

J: How are you feeling toward that Sheep Part now?

A: I'm feeling great affection toward it. [laughs]

J: OK, good.

A: But I also notice, when I tune into that part, that I have a low-grade headache. I can feel this energy around my head that's muffling it—that's making me numb, or something. I don't think it's just from hitting things. It's almost like turning down my awareness somehow, turning down my sensitivity— like a numbing kind of feeling.

J: So invite that part to tell you what it wants or what its concerns are.

A: It says it wants everybody to leave me the hell alone. It says I'm better off by myself. I could just hang out with nature and feel really filled up and balanced. It wants me to just hang out with my own inner system and not have to deal with other people at all. That's what it wants for me.

J: Ask the part what it's afraid that other people will do to you that makes it want to get away from them.

A: I get an image of being a little kid and having all these big people screaming at me, right in my ears. It's like this horrible static on the line all the time— really, really loud. I can't hear myself think, there's so much interference. I can't feel myself, either.

J: It sounds like this part is really concerned about other people keeping you from feeling yourself. Is that right?

A: Yeah. I'm getting an image of this little girl who's covering her ears and her head, trying to protect herself, trying to turn all that craziness off ... I'm having some sadness come up.

J: Is this little girl the same part, or a different one?

A: It feels like it's the exile that the Sheep Part is protecting. Like the exile is so overwhelmed by all this noisy, chaotic input from other people.

When Anne asked the Sheep Part what it was afraid of, she not only discovered its positive intent, she also accessed the exile it is protecting.

J: And when you see her, you feel sad.

A: Yeah.

J: And is this her sadness, or are you sad *for* her?

A: I'm sad *for* her.

J: OK, and the Sheep Part is really trying to protect her ...

A: Yeah.

J: ... from this interference and shouting from other people.

A: And it's violence, too. It's not just noise. It's physical abuse.

The Sheep Part is trying to protect Anne from anger and violence that she experienced as a child.

J: So ask the Sheep Part to tell you how it goes about trying to protect her.

A: It makes it so when I'm with other people it feels really stressful, and when I'm by myself it feels really nice and peaceful. The Sheep Part makes it much more extreme than it would be otherwise.

J: It makes your experience of other people more stressful.

A: Yeah.

J: Ask it how it does that.

A: It makes me believe that my energy is getting drained when I'm with other people. And it makes me feel really tired and have this craving to be alone.

J: See if there's anything else that the Sheep Part wants you to know about itself.

A: It's rather hostile. It says, "I'm never going to let you be with other people. I'm always going to keep you in this place."

J: So it's feeling hostile toward you?

A: Yeah, like "Don't mess with this." The Sheep Part is saying, "I'm in charge—I'm going to keep it that way. Don't try to tweak the system at all."

J: Uh-huh. Ask it what it's afraid you're going to try to do that makes it feel hostile toward you.

A: It's afraid that my life's purpose is going to override its wishes—that my Life Purpose Part is so strong that it's going to win out in the end.

J: So it's feeling hostile because it's afraid that without that anger, the other part will take over, and it won't be able to protect the little girl part.

A: Yeah, and it feels kind of like ... There's this really interesting feel to it. The Sheep Part feels like it has to get really mean and bitchy. It understands that the Life Purpose Part is really sweet, and it doesn't want to let that sweetness win out. So the emotions of the two are really polarized as well.

J: Ask the Sheep Part what would happen if the sweetness won out.

A: People would be naturally drawn to me.

J: And if they were drawn to you, what is it afraid would happen?

A: Then I'd have a lot of people around me, and they'd start screaming and being abusive and mean—treating me badly.

Notice how the polarization is making the Sheep Part more extreme. It believes that it must be hostile to counter the Life Purpose Part so it can protect that wounded exile.

J: I can hear that you're really feeling some of the pain that comes from being screamed at. That's probably some of the exile's pain.

A: Yeah.

J: I can certainly see why the Sheep Part would feel the need be so protective, if that's what it's trying to protect you from.

A: Yeah.

J: Do you need to do some separating from the exile, or are you still pretty much in Self?

A: I feel OK—I'm in Self.

At this point, Anne was feeling some of the exile's pain, so I checked with her to see if she was too blended with this exile, or if it was OK with her. She is solidly enough in Self that she can feel this much of the exile's pain without a problem, so we can safely go on.

J: It sounds like you're appreciating that the Sheep Part intends to protect the exile.

A: Yeah. Definitely.

J: So let it know that you appreciate what it's trying to do.

A: I just got this really strong hit that this Sheep Part doesn't want to do its job anymore. It's like it's grown these giant horns, and it's got a headache from them and from pushing everything away all the time. But it's really scared of the exile getting hurt. And it's also concerned about being seen as bad, even though I don't see it as bad.

Once the Sheep Part felt Anne's appreciation, it relaxed its rigid attachment to its role. This is probably because it now realizes that Self is there to help with the danger it perceives. Once it relaxed, it realized that it was tired of its job.

J: So even though you don't see it as bad, there may be some other parts of you that do. So it's concerned about that?

A: And people in my life who think that my distancing behavior is a really bad thing.

J: Sure, that would make sense. Because it's partly designed to make them feel that way so they won't get too close to you, right?

A: Yeah.

J: You might let the Sheep Part know that we're working on making it safe enough so it could let go of its job if it wanted to.

A: This part feels like it's kind of between a rock and a hard place. It really wants to give up that function, but it's *really* afraid for the exile. However, now it really feels my support, like it's not just stuck by itself with this dilemma. It's got some help.

This shows the importance of developing a relationship between Self and each polarized part. Once they feel connected to Self, they're much more amenable to learning to cooperate with each other.

This transcript will continue later in the book. It illustrates one of the biggest advantages of using IFS to resolve polarization. There are other therapy methods that include dialogue between polarized parts, but they simply have the parts talk to each other. IFS adds to this its understanding of the importance of the Self and of having each polarized part connected with the Self before starting the dialogue. This makes a huge difference.

Chapter 6

Deciding Which Approach to Use

ONCE THE CLIENT HAS CONNECTED WITH EACH POLAR-
ized part, you can proceed toward depolarizing the
situation and promoting cooperation between the parts.

Remember that each polarized protector is locked into
its extreme role for two reasons: (1) It is protecting an exile,
and (2) It is polarized with a part it thinks is dangerous.
Therefore, there are two choices for how to resolve the situation (though in many cases, you may have to do both):

1. Unburden the exile (or exiles) being protected by one
part or both parts. Then help the protectors to let go of
their protective roles so they can get along with each other.
To the extent that one of the protectors is extreme because
it is protecting a very vulnerable or traumatized exile, it
probably won't let go until the exile is healed. Therefore,
following the ordinary IFS approach, you get permission
from the protector to access this exile and then follow the
steps to get to know the exile, witness the origins of its
burden, and reparent, retrieve, and unburden it. After this,
you help the protector to relax and let go of its role.

I won't discuss this procedure in detail in this book,
except to show how it relates to polarization work. If you
aren't familiar with how to work with exiles, you can read
chapters 10–15 of my book *Self-Therapy*.

2. Facilitate a depolarization dialogue between the two parts. This helps them to learn how to cooperate rather than fight each other. How to facilitate this dialogue is discussed in the rest of this book.

It is worth mentioning that it is sometimes useful to have two parts talk to each other, even if they aren't polarized. For example, in the case of an inner critic part and a part that is receiving the criticism and feeling bad, I have sometimes found it useful to introduce these parts to each other because the critic often doesn't know about the pain it is causing.

How to Decide Which Approach to Use

Step 4 in the polarization process involves deciding which approach to use. Sometimes a polarization seems to be caused mainly by the extreme behavior or feelings of one protector, and the other side is mostly a correction or an attempt to deal with this situation. Usually the extremes of this part come from its dire need to protect an exile, so it makes sense to unburden that exile first. Then you check to see if that protector can become less extreme or even let go of its role. This process may resolve the polarization. Even if it doesn't, healing this exile will make it easier to resolve the polarization using dialogue.

Let's look at the example of a client who has a polarization between a Taskmaster Part that is pushing him to work very hard and a Procrastinator Part that is trying to avoid doing work that it finds threatening. Suppose you sense that the Procrastinator is intense because of its fear of taking on this task and failing. It is protecting an exile who was judged or humiliated when the client was young.

In this case, you probably won't get much traction until this exile is healed and the Procrastinator can let go.

On the other hand, sometimes it seems that the main driving force behind the polarization is the two parts trying to counter each other. This doesn't mean that both parts aren't also protecting exiles, but rather that they are primarily focused on countering each other, and this is where the polarization comes from. In this case, it makes sense to start with the depolarization dialogue. Helping the two parts to cooperate may resolve the polarization without needing to heal the exiles, or it may create a more congenial internal relationship, which will make it easier to access and heal the exiles.

For example, let's imagine a different polarized situation between a Taskmaster and Procrastinator. Suppose that, rather than intense procrastination, the situation is more of a battle between a Taskmaster Part that really is pushing too hard and a Procrastinator that is fighting back against the extreme push. Suppose, in addition, that you sense that the Taskmaster's overblown desire to succeed is modeled after an extremely pushy father and is designed to protect against his judgments. You may know from other work you have done with this client that the exile being protected—the one who was hurt by the father—isn't extremely wounded. Then it would make sense to begin with a depolarization dialogue rather than exile work.

In some cases, two parts are primarily fighting each other because the client grew up in a highly charged, polarized environment, and he or she is recreating that external environment internally.

When you are getting to know a protector, here is one way to tell whether it is more concerned about the exile it is protecting or the part it is polarized with. Ask the protector the usual IFS question, "What are you afraid would happen if you didn't (do your job)?" If the protector says, "I'm afraid you'll feel humiliated" (or some other painful feeling), this points to an exile who feels humiliated. If it says, "I'm afraid you'll be judged" (or harmed in some other way), this points to an exile who was judged. Both of these situations indicate that the protector is primarily concerned about this exile, and it might be better to start by healing it.

However, if the protector says, "I'm afraid you'll fly off the handle" (or some other destructive behavior), this points to the polarized part because it is that part that might engage in the feared behavior. This probably indicates that the protector is primarily concerned about countering its polarized part, and it might be better to start with a depolarization dialogue.

No matter which approach you start with, you may want to use the other as well, so it may not matter in the end where you start. For example, in some cases even if you start with the depolarization dialogue, you will still need to heal the exiles being protected in order to resolve the polarization. Or even if you don't *have* to heal them to resolve the polarization, it would still be helpful to heal them at some point for the client's greater well-being.

And on the other hand, even if you start by healing one or both exiles, you may still need to engage in the depolarization dialogue to fully resolve the polarization.

Chapter 7

Getting Permission for a Depolarization Dialogue

I F YOU DECIDE ON A DIALOGUE, YOU MOVE TO STEP 5, GET-ting permission from both parts for the dialogue. Have the client ask each part, one at a time, if it would be willing to have a dialogue with the other part in order to resolve the conflict. Make it clear that the dialogue will take place under the guidance of the client (in Self) with your help. You might ask each part if it is aware of the work you did with the other part. If so, that will help them to be more open to dialoguing with each other.

In many cases, both parts will agree to the dialogue because of the preliminary work you have already done in having the client develop a trusting relationship with each of them. However, if either part isn't willing, have the client ask what it is afraid will happen in the dialogue. Then the client can reassure the part that he or she won't let anything destructive occur.

Here are some common fears that polarized parts have about engaging in a dialogue, along with how to handle each one:

1. One part is afraid that the other part will take over the client and do dangerous things. For example, one part

might be afraid that the other part will get enraged if it is let out of the box it has been kept it. Have the client explain that he or she will stay in Self and won't let the other part take over. You can add that you will be there to help, if necessary. Of course, you don't mean that you or the Self will *prohibit* the other part from taking over. We never use force with parts in IFS. What you mean is that your orientation will be toward the client staying in Self, and if the other part does take over, you will help the client to unblend. You can add that by engaging in the depolarization dialogue, the polarized part will be less likely to do anything dangerous.

2. One part is afraid to talk to the other part for fear of being attacked by it. For example, one part might be afraid that an Inner Critic Part will start judging the client or the part. Explain that you and the client will be in charge of the dialogue and that if the other part attacks, you will ask what it is afraid of that makes it attack, thus shifting the conversation in a different direction. You will be encouraging each part to learn to cooperate with the other. Remind the scared part that the client has already connected with the other part safely earlier in the session.

3. One part doesn't want to talk to the other part because it feels that the dialogue would legitimize the other part. Part A believes that Part B is so evil that it shouldn't be given any airtime. It wants to completely dismiss Part B and have nothing to do with it. Explain that Part B has a positive intent for the client and therefore deserves to be heard. Also make it clear that ostracizing Part B cannot work because it will just operate out of the client's awareness and do more damage. Furthermore, the dialogue

will result in a new cooperative situation in which Part B won't take destructive action any more.

If necessary, use your authority as therapist and the client's trust in you to help him or her get permission. Explain that you have experience with this kind of dialogue and you know what you are doing. Reassure the parts that you will be in charge and won't let anything destructive happen.

You have a solid foundation for the dialogue because of the work the client has already done in getting to know each part and discovering its positive intent. While this was happening, the client found out how each part was trying to help and how it was trying to protect a wounded exile.

In addition, the other polarized part was usually listening in the background. (Parts do this.) It also discovered that the first part, which it thought was totally evil and destructive, was actually trying to protect a hurt child part. This understanding helps to break down the animosity between the parts. Each part begins to see that the other part is really trying to help the client. So even though they each think that the opposing part is causing problems, they are likely to be more open to each other and more willing to dialogue.

For example, Dan's Drink Controller at first hated the Drinker because it was causing serious trouble in Dan's life. However, it overheard Dan's work with the Drinker and found out that it was trying to protect a wounded little boy who had been severely rejected by his mother. As a result, the Drink Controller softened its stance toward the Drinker. It realized that the Drinker was doing its best to cope with devastating pain, and that made it more open to dialoguing with the Drinker.

If one part won't give permission, this may indicate that you need to work more on the client's relationship with this part. It may not have developed enough trust in Self for the dialogue to be successful. Have the client ask the part if it doesn't trust him or her, and then work on the trust issue. Or check to see if the client really appreciates the part and if the part understands that. If this isn't the case, spend more time supporting the client to truly understand and appreciate the part, or work on the part being able to take in the appreciation.

Chapter 8

Beginning the
Depolarization Dialogue

O NCE THE CLIENT HAS THE PERMISSION OF BOTH PARTS,
it is time to arrange the depolarization dialogue and
begin, which is Step 6 in the process.

Setting Up the Dialogue

There are three ways to set up the dialogue—externally, in
an inner space, or a mix of the two.

Externally. This setup is done in a way that was pio-
neered by Gestalt Therapy. It is considered a form of
"direct access" in IFS because the therapist talks directly
to parts (and they talk to each other). You arrange three
(or more) chairs or pillows, two representing each part
and one representing the Self.

When it is time for one part to speak, the client sits in
that chair and embodies the part or plays the role of the
part. Another way to say this is that the client consciously
blends with that part. This is different from normal blending where the client is usually unaware of being blended
with a part. In this case, the client consciously chooses to
blend with the part, which means that he or she won't
be overwhelmed by its feelings and won't buy into its

worldview. The client becomes the part in the moment but retains his or her larger sense of perspective.

The client speaks out loud as the part. He or she looks at the other chair and directs the conversation to the other part as if it's sitting in the empty chair. Then the client switches seats, becomes the other part, and responds by speaking out loud back to the first part. You coach the client about when to switch chairs and sometimes what to say. Whenever it seems helpful, you direct him or her to occupy the Self chair and speak as Self to facilitate the dialogue. If the client is having trouble staying unblended, you might have him or her sit in the Self chair for a moment after each part speaks to reaccess Self.

The advantage of this approach is that it is easy for the client to access and identify with each part. Every part comes really alive, and its feelings and beliefs are natural for the client to understand. It is also easier for the client to experience them speaking with each other. Clients rarely get the parts mixed up. This approach is especially helpful for clients who have poor access to parts or who tend to get their parts muddled. Such clients may have trouble telling one part from the other or may skip from one part to another without realizing it. This external approach helps such clients to maintain clarity about their parts.

The disadvantage of the external approach is that the Self may not be as easily accessible, and accidental blending may occur. Since the client is consciously blending with each part, the Self isn't simultaneously present with the part. When you are facilitating an internal dialogue, the client is in Self when he or she is listening to the parts converse with each other. This makes it easier for the client to stay in Self and not get too blended with either part.

Internally. The client brings the two parts together in an inner space where they can talk to each other. This could be visual—for example, seeing the two parts sitting in a room together or at a conference table. Or the client could just sense the parts in a place where they can communicate with each other. When each part speaks, the client hears what it says internally and reports on this to you.

The client must also be present in the inner space as Self so she can facilitate the dialogue. However, make sure that the client doesn't see an image of herself in the internal space. Any image the client sees is not Self. Self is the observer—the subject—never the object. If the client sees an image of herself speaking to a part, this is another part the client is seeing, not Self. Instead of seeing the Self in the space, the client should just feel herself in the space.

The advantage of this internal approach is that the client is simultaneously in Self and with a part all the time, so there can more easily be a strong Self presence. The disadvantage is that some clients may have a harder time accessing their parts or may mix them up without the clarity that comes from having a chair for each part.

Mixture. The client arranges the internal dialogue as above, and she also sits in two different chairs externally as each part is speaking inside. This approach helps the client to access each part more clearly and to keep them differentiated. There are a variety of ways to mix external and internal work, so feel free to use your creativity in deciding on the best approach for each client.

Beginning the Conversation

Either part can begin the dialogue by speaking to the other part. Occasionally one part may want to speak to the Self first, but then direct it to speak to the other part. At first, the parts will probably just state and argue their existing positions, which is fine. It will give the client (and you) a clear understanding of the polarization and how each part is reacting to and countering the other one.

However, don't allow them to attack each other. This would interfere with the development of real dialogue. Furthermore, you have promised them that you won't allow attacks to happen. It's important to hold to this promise so the parts don't lose trust in you or the client.

At this point in the process, the two parts are often locked into their polarized stances and are arguing with each other. This isn't true dialogue, but it's OK to start this way.

At this point in the process, it can sometimes be helpful to ask the parts to show which people in the client's life are aligned with each part. This gives you a feel for how the polarization dynamics plays out in the client's life.

Sometimes you may be surprised to discover that the parts are already moving into true dialogue. Because of the preliminary work you have done to have the client connect with and develop trust with each part, the parts are more likely to be ready to cooperate. In addition, each part may have learned about the other part's positive intent and the fact that it is protecting a vulnerable exile. This understanding often softens them toward each other.

The parts are especially likely to cooperate if both of them are trying to protect the same exile. Before this polarization work, they wouldn't have that understanding, but once they do, they tend to feel connected to each other, even if they are using opposing strategies to protect the exile.

Chapter 9

True Dialogue and Resolution

O NCE EACH POLARIZED PART HAS STATED ITS POSITION clearly through a couple of rounds of back-and-forth conversation, you can begin to facilitate an actual dialogue between them. This is Step 7 in the polarization process. It is handled in a way that is similar to mediation and conflict resolution between people.

Facilitating True Dialogue

It is helpful if each part states its positive intent for the client and what exile it is trying to protect. Sharing this information makes the other part more receptive to it. Sometimes the parts will spontaneously do this during the early stages of the dialogue, but if they don't, ask them to do so. This begins to move the conversation beyond simply taking positions.

For example, suppose Sandra's Family Part is arguing that she must go to a family reunion, while her Safety Part is adamant about not going. The Family Part initially just argues that a good person stays in touch with his or her family. Ask it to tell the other part what it is trying to get for Sandra, such as love and acceptance from certain family member. Or ask it to explain what exile it is protecting, perhaps one who was not fully accepted in her family.

At some point, intervene and ask one part to actually listen to what the other part is saying before it responds. You might even ask it to acknowledge what the other part has said. Then ask it to respond in a way that takes into account what is important to the other part. It doesn't have to agree with the other part; it just needs to listen to it and respond in a way that respects the other part's concerns.

For example, when Sandra's Safety Part says that it doesn't think it's safe to go to the family reunion because it's afraid she will be ridiculed, ask the Family Part to really listen to this fear. When it responds, it might say, "I understand that you are afraid of being ridiculed, but I don't think that is likely to happen. And I think it is so important to stay connected with your family that it is worth the risk." Here the part is still advocating its position, but it is responding to the Safety Part's concerns.

Then ask the other part to do the same thing. This marks the beginning of real dialogue, which means that two parts (or people) are authentically listening to each other. The process also begins to access the healthy side of each part, or the Self within each part. (IFS recognizes that each part can have Self within it. This is what you want to bring to the fore in this dialogue.)

This movement toward cooperation is aided by the presence of the therapist in Self and the energy of the client in Self. It isn't just the interventions that make a difference but the quality of your presence and your openness to both parts.

The Relationship Between the Parts and the Self

If one or both parts aren't willing to move past fighting and toward dialogue, it may be an indication that they don't trust the client's Self enough. In that case, you may need to go back and work more on the relationship between the Self and one (or both) of the parts.

If one part (or Self) doesn't understand something that is important to the other part, you need to intervene as therapist and point this out. Make sure that each part has really heard and taken into account the other part's position.

You are aiming for the two parts to begin to cooperate with each other. After all, they each want something positive for the client, and they are stuck with each other. Neither one can get rid of the other. They both should be aware of this by now, even though they may not have realized it at first. So it is in their best interests (as well as the client's) for them to learn to cooperate. In fact, it is usually possible for both parts to get all or most of what they want if they cooperate.

You have a good chance of convincing the parts to really listen to each other because of the preliminary work you have done in helping the client to access Self, get to know each part, and develop a trusting relationship with it. This creates a sense of safety for each part because they now realize that there is a larger, caring force present in the client's psyche—the Self. They have connected with the Self and they know that the Self respects them and takes their concerns seriously. So they are usually open to listening to the other part and attempting to cooperate with it because the Self is asking them to do this and is reassuring them that it won't let anything destructive happen.

The presence of the Self and its relationship with each part is what makes IFS polarization work so powerful in contrast to other therapy methods that involve internal dialogue.

Resolution

Resolving the polarization can take two different forms. The two parts are often disagreeing over a specific action they each want the client to take. One level of resolution is deciding what to do or how to handle a particular situation. However, a deeper and more important kind of resolution takes place when the two parts learn to appreciate each other and cooperate with each other. This kind will have a larger impact because it will influence future decisions and feelings that have to do with the split between these parts.

Resolutions of either kind can occur at any step in the process. Sometimes just getting to know the two parts from Self will produce a resolution. Sometimes the very beginning of the dialogue will do that. At other times, you get this far in the dialogue, and there is still no resolution. Then the client can step in as Self to help get there. If you are facilitating the dialogue externally, have the client switch into a third chair that represents Self. If you are doing it internally, have the client speak from the place of Self.

The Self might notice that one part is ignoring a crucial aspect of what's bothering the other part, and therefore the other part is still arguing in an extreme way because it doesn't feel heard. For example, John had a Taskmaster Part that was worried that his Fun Part would cause him to get fired from his job. The Fun Part only saw that the Taskmaster was concerned about his not being successful enough. John (in Self) pointed out the Taskmaster's more extreme fear to the Fun Part so it could be dealt with.

The Self might see a way that the two parts are similar, which they are completely missing because of their adversarial stance with each other. For example, they both might be protecting the same exile.

If appropriate, have the client ask each part to suggest a solution that takes into account the other part's concerns and needs. If this doesn't produce anything, the client can offer a solution from Self. After observing the dialogue, the client can sometimes see a resolution from Self that would be agreeable to both parts.

If the client doesn't see a resolution, you can offer one. Sometimes you have a better perspective on the situation than the client's Self has. You can offer this perspective or even offer a solution. However, don't get attached to your solution. It's just one step in the negotiating process. And you often don't know the whole story.

Negotiating a Resolution

Encourage the client to offer a solution and see if both parts will agree to it. Even if they don't immediately agree, this can shift the dialogue in a fruitful direction. If either part doesn't agree, have the client ask what its concerns are, and then modify the solution to take them into account. Or ask the part to offer a modified version of the solution. Keep negotiating until you have a solution that is acceptable to both parts.

This process can sometimes take quite a bit of time as each part considers each possible solution and discusses its concerns. Sometimes one of the parts (or Self) will suggest a new, creative idea that hasn't been considered before. This is one of the benefits of having this kind of cooperative dialogue. It helps to access the positive qualities and creativity of each part.

If you keep the dialogue going as the parts negotiate about a proposed solution, they are very likely to arrive at something that will work for both of them and, of course, for the client. After all, they both want the best for the client, so when they are fully cooperating under the guidance of the Self and the therapist, a solution is bound to come. During the dialogue, a part may reveal the exile it is protecting, and sometimes it becomes clear that this exile must be healed for the polarization to be resolved.

The entire process of working with polarization often takes multiple sessions. You have to get to know each polarized part separately before you can begin the dialogue. That in itself can take an entire session, or even more. Then the dialogue might need to go through a number of phases. In addition, the client may need to try out a proposed solution in his or her life to see what happens. Doing this often brings up unresolved issues that must be dealt with in future sessions. During this process, it is helpful to remind the client at the beginning of each session to reengage this work from the point at which it stopped in the previous session.

If the two parts aren't ready to come to a resolution in a particular session, ask them to agree to one step toward cooperation that works for both of them. You can then return to take further steps in later sessions.

For particularly recalcitrant parts, the best initial outcome may be for each of them to realize that the ways they are currently operating aren't working. They may not yet be ready to resolve the situation with the opposing part. However, when they realize that their current strategies aren't working, it opens them up to rethink their calcified positions. This can lead to greater attention to each part's relationship with the Self or work on the exile being protected. A more productive dialogue can then emerge in the future.

Appendix A contains a Help Sheet that outlines all the steps of the IFS procedure for working with polarization. It can be used to guide you in a session.

Chapter 10

Anne's Depolarization Dialogue

THIS IS A CONTINUATION OF THE POLARIZATION SESSION with Anne from Chapter 5. It shows Steps 5–7 of the polarization process. This particular segment illustrates how the parts can move into a cooperative mode with each other as well as the importance of healing an exile to promote depolarization.

J: See if the Sheep Part would be willing to have a dialogue with the Life Purpose Part.

A: [laughs] It says it will if I hold its hand. It wants to make sure it stays in touch with me. It doesn't want to be out there by itself.

J: Is that OK with you?

A: Yeah, it's fine.

This hand-holding is an indication of the valuable work Anne has already done in connecting with each part and developing a trusting relationship.

J: Check with the Life Purpose Part and see if it's willing to have a dialogue with the Sheep.

A: It wants to hold my other hand. [laughs] It's like, "I'm not going to let that other part have one of your hands if I can't have the other one. We've got to keep this even."

J: So I guess they're kind of already in a space where they can talk to each other, if they're each holding your hand.

Since they are already in contact internally, I don't bother to ask her to choose the internal versus external setup.

A: Yeah. They're sitting across from each other, making funny, mean faces at each other.

J: Invite them to start talking to each other, and either one of them can begin. And let us know what they're actually saying.

A: Well, the Sheep Part is saying to the Life Purpose Part, "You're going way too fast. We have to slow this whole thing down. You're trying to make something happen that just isn't ready to happen yet."

The Life Purpose Part is saying, "I've been waiting all my life! How much longer do we have to wait for this?" And it's also saying, "Anne's not going live forever, so at some point we've got to get this show on the road."

J: OK. Let the dialogue continue, and keep letting us know what they're saying.

A: The Sheep Part says, "She's way too fragile for what you have in mind for her." Which tells me that the Sheep Part is confusing *me* with the exile—that the Sheep Part doesn't get that I'm an adult and I'm really capable now.

It's often the case that a part confuses the person with another part. Sometimes, as in this case, a protector sees the person as an exile. At other times, a polarized part sees the person as the other polarized part.

J: Why don't you say that to the Sheep Part and see how it responds to you?

A: Well, it says that I have that exile inside of me, and she could get stirred up at any moment. So it understands that I'm not *really* the exile, but the exile's just under the surface.

J: So it still needs to protect her.

A: Yeah.

This is an important step toward true dialogue. When one part reveals the exile it's protecting, that tends to soften the other part because it realizes that the first part isn't all bad—it's trying to protect the client from pain. This makes the other part more open to the first part.

J: Ask the Life Purpose Part to take a moment to take in what the Sheep Part is saying. It doesn't have to agree, but just take it in.

I do this to shift the conversation in the direction of dialogue rather than argument.

A: OK, it's done that.

J: Now let it respond in a way that takes the Sheep Part's concerns into account.

A: Well, the Life Purpose Part actually got concerned about that exile. Like, "Oh, somebody here is in a lot of pain." It's not about these two parts anymore. It's about this Little Girl who's in pain. The Life Purpose Part doesn't want to do anything that's going to hurt the Little Girl.

It's possible that there are other exiles in addition to the Little Girl who are being protected by the Sheep Part.

A: It's really interesting. I just saw the Little Girl come into this circle. The other two parts each took one of her hands, and she's sitting in the circle. So now it's the four of us. And the Little Girl is kind of curled up and looking down, but it feels important that she's part of the circle now.

Both of the protectors say they want to help her. This is really sweet. [laughs] And the Sheep just took off its horns and put them on the little girl and said, "You want to try on a little Halloween costume here?"

The little girl is laughing, but she says, "No, it's way too heavy for *my* head!" But the Sheep isn't real angry and harsh anymore.

This is a big shift. The parts are really dialoguing and beginning to cooperate.

J: Certainly an important part of the resolution of this issue will be doing the healing work with that Little Girl. However, let's keep going with this dialogue and see how far these two can get in terms of deciding what to do about this life purpose project that you want to do.

A: It doesn't feel like they're in opposition anymore. It feels like they're both in agreement that the exile needs some help and that nothing else should happen until that happens. I don't mean that has to happen today, since I know we're nearly out of time. But the Life Purpose Part is on board with the agenda of taking care of the exile instead of just pushing forward with my other goals. And the Sheep Part is very happy about this.

J: Ask the Sheep Part the following: If we healed the Little Girl of her pain and fear so she was safe, would it still need to keep you away from people?

A: It says that would be a great relief. It's really tired of its role, and it's sick and tired of being judged as bad by other people. It would be happy to take a break if the Little Girl were truly safe.

J: Great. And how does the Life Purpose Part feel about that?

A: It says that it's about time. When the Little Girl is healed, it's ready to take over and get me out in the world making a difference.

J: So maybe this is a good place to stop for today.

The two parts are now fully cooperating, and the next thing that needs to happen is healing the Little Girl. This can be done using the regular IFS procedure. This part of the session illustrates both aspects of resolving polarization—exile healing and depolarization dialogue—and how they can work together.

A: Yeah, I feel fine to do that.

J: So just check and see if any of those parts want to say anything before we stop.

A: Nope, they all seem pretty content.

J: See if there's anything you want to say to any of them.

A: I'm just thanking all of them and saying we'll get together again. I'll visit them before long and see what wants to happen next.

It isn't usually quite this easy to achieve cooperation between polarized parts, but it does happen.

Chapter 11

Nancy's Depolarization Dialogue

HIS IS THE TRANSCRIPT OF A SESSION WITH NANCY IN A polarization class. It shows Steps 5–7 of the polarization process. This particular session illustrates a number of important processes that didn't come up in Anne's session. Nancy works with her dialogue externally, including some "direct access" of the parts by me. The session also illustrates a situation that requires a lot of work for the polarized parts to achieve resolution, even though they are willing to cooperate with each other. I have to intervene with suggestions a number of times, including an idea for achieving a resolution.

Nancy had worked on this issue in a previous demo in this class, so she wasn't starting from scratch with these parts. This allowed us to move right to the dialogue.

J: So describe your parts. Even if these are the ones you've already worked on in a previous demo, describe them again so we're all on board.

N: There basically seem to be three parts. It's like a three-way polarization, but two of them are on one side, and one's on the other side. So there's the exile, which is the Kid who wants to just go with every thought, be spontaneous, have fun, play, and not be boxed in by plans and schedules and having to work.

Then there's the active Procrastinator, which acts on the Kid's desires by avoiding work and trying to have fun. And that part is polarized with a part that says, "You have to work. Work is real. You have to go make the stuff. You have to ship it out. You have to stop procrastinating." It's a heavy-handed Work Ethic Part. It's polarized with the side that includes the Kid and the Procrastinator.

A polarization can contain more than two parts. There can be any number of parts on each side.

J: OK, and you say they have already been dialoguing.

N: Yeah, they have been dialoguing a number of times.

J: Do you feel you've made a good connection with each of them?

N: Yeah, when I have the dialogues, there's a reasonable amount of understanding all the way around between the parts. I understand the intelligence of the parts and the reactivity of the parts. I see the intelligence of the Kid, the Procrastinator, and the Work Ethic Part I can see what they each have to offer.

J: Let's work with them one at a time. We'll access each one and get their permission to have another dialogue.

N: OK, so I've accessed the work one, the Work Ethic Part

J: And see if that part's willing to dialogue.

N: Yeah, it's willing to dialogue.

J: OK, now access one of the others.

N: OK, I'm accessing the Kid Part, the spontaneous one.

J: OK, see if that one's willing to dialogue.

N: Yeah, it's willing to dialogue.

J: And the third one?

N: And the protector of the Kid—the Procrastinator. Yeah, I can access that one, and it's willing to dialogue.

Now Nancy has permission from all three parts for the dialogue. This was easy to achieve since she had previously connected with each of the parts.

J: And do you want to do this dialogue internally or externally?

N: I've got to do it externally.

J: So set up four chairs, one for each of those three parts plus one for Self.

N: OK. I have three chairs and a table. The Kid can sit on the table.

J: Any one of them can start. So whichever one wants to start, just sit in that part's chair, and speak to the part or parts on the other side of the polarization.

N: So I'm in the chair of the Work Ethic Part, and I'm speaking to the Kid and the Procrastinator. And my feeling at this point is, I'm tired. I'm tired of the battle we get into every day, but I really feel at a loss to give up my position because stores are calling in with lots of orders, even in these times of economic difficulty. That seems really wonderful, and these orders really need to get done in a timely way. But I really feel like you guys sabotage that.

Even with the banks collapsing, and nobody knowing who's going to have a good Christmas in stores, you guys still don't pay any attention. You keep me from working in an organized, efficient way. And the effect of that is you make the orders late, and you don't allow the work to get ahead. I wish people could call in and instantly have their orders filled, rather than having to wait a week or two for the stuff to be made.

I have envisioned that the whole thing would be much more stress-free if it could be organized and if stuff could be made ahead of time and shipped out right when people call in. It seems like everybody—all of us and the store—would be so happy if they called in and you said, "Oh, I could just ship that out right now," as opposed to saying a week or two or three. But I'm mostly just tired and at a loss for how to work with this so that your sabotaging doesn't keep taking place. That's the Work Ethic Part.

J: Sounds good. So switch over to one of the other parts and let them respond.

N: Now I'm in the Procrastinator protector chair. I understand that you have a lot of concern for orders and money and getting the stuff out. It does sound nice, that people would call in and you could say,

"I'll get that right out." That seems like it would be a lot of fun and cheerful and stress-free.

Notice that the Procrastinator already shows some understanding of the Work Ethic Part's position. This is good.

But our position over here is: We just feel like you'll always have us working. We have no sense that you really understand that we need space, that we need playtime, we need creative-space time.

We don't think you'll ever give it to us because you have infinite plans. You really just get off on plans. We look at that and go, "Oh my god. It's going to be plans and stuff to do till we're dead. We won't get to enjoy the trees and greenery and garden puttering; we won't have any fun! So we figure we're just going to take it now! 'Cause we like instant gratification. And we don't trust that you'll ever give us any space and playtime.

J: I'm thinking to switch back and hear what the Work Ethic part has to say to that, but I don't want to leave out the Kid if the Kid needs to say something.

N: No, the Kid's fine, the Kid's sitting on the table swinging her legs, like, "La la la. This is fine." No, the Procrastinator is definitely speaking on behalf of the Kid. It's the protector, so the Kid's fine.

J: So switch back to the Work Ethic part.

N as Work Ethic Part: I'm getting the picture that you don't trust me. You don't trust that I will give you any space or time to play or have fun. Or that if I do, it'll be so minimal compared to what you want that it's not enough. I see we have a discrepancy here. You want more time and space than I feel I can give.

The Work Ethic Part also has an understanding of the Procrastinator's position. Their understanding of each other will make it easier to get a resolution.

I can see we don't really trust each other. You want a lot of time and space, and I want a lot of work. I'm willing to give you *some* time and space and see how that goes. And I have this feeling that if we could really work without your distractions, then time might be more efficient. And maybe more would get done.

But there's something you said about plans. You're right, I like planning. And to me that's part of the creativity of ideas. So I take issue with your thing about the planning. I think some of the planning is a way to get around all the sabotaging that you do, and some of the planning is creative idea hatching. So I'd just like to put this out there: I might not have to do so much of the heavy-handed planning if I could trust that you wouldn't sabotage me.

I understand you want more playtime. I'm definitely willing to give playtime space.

J: Let me just jump in a little, and remind you, as the Work Ethic Part, that they didn't say they wanted *more* playtime. They said they don't believe that you're going to ever give them *any*. That's what their impression was.

I noticed that the Work Ethic Part had missed a crucial aspect of the Procrastinator's fears.

N as Work Ethic Part: OK, I understand. So how about if I give you *some*. I understand you don't trust me to give you any, so you're taking as much as you can. So if we can come to an agreement where I actually give you some, and absolutely stick to it . . .

I can feel that I have a hesitancy in saying "absolutely stick to it" because what we *have* to do something and I've said it's playtime? So I can feel my hesitancy in giving up that kind of authority, in saying, "Well, if we work from 9 to 12 and 1 to 4 filling kilns, will I really stop at 4?"

This is important. The Work Ethic Part is really recognizing what would be involved in sticking to this agreement, and it is considering whether it is willing to. What usually happens is that one side comes up with a plan and tries to institute it without getting the informed consent of the other side. This is sure to backfire. However, if both sides think through an agreement and decide to abide by it, then it can work.

The agreement we worked out with Self was to try kiln loading in the basement from 9 to 12, take a break from 12 to 1, then jewelry, kiln making from 1 to 4, then break at 4 for puttering and play stuff. I'm willing to try it, but if something came up, then I would just have to say, "No, I can't do that at four o'clock." But if I didn't agree to playtime at 4, I can understand that would breed a lack of trust in you, and you'd say, "Ha! Told you so."

J: So it seems like if you back out on your agreement, they're just going to really not trust you, and they're going to sabotage things all the more.

N as Self: Right, but I can see the fear in this Work Ethic Part. Committing to not working from 4 to 6 is pretty scary, so I don't know what to do about that.

J: So what are you scared of, Work Ethic Part?

The Work Ethic Part is scared to make the agreement, so I ask what it is scared of. Notice that I am speaking to the part using "direct access."

N as Work Ethic Part: I'm afraid that there'll be important work that has to happen and that it won't happen. I mean, yeah, it could be put off till the next day, so I guess that's what I have to be willing to do. Or it could be put off till six o'clock. I guess that I'll be willing to do that. It's like I could say I could do that for a day, but on a regular basis I can't do that.

J: But don't forget, if you do this, they're agreeing to stop sabotaging you. So you're going to get a lot done from 9 to 12 and 1 to 4 if you stick to this. You have a lot to gain by sticking to this. Because they're agreeing to not sabotage you anymore.

I am attempting to show the Work Ethic Part what it has to gain by agreeing.

N as Work Ethic Part: Right. But I can see their point that there will always be work to do. I really do feel that there's an enormous amount of work. So I need more hours than six hours a day. Yes, I can work in the evenings, which I do, but there's stuff that comes up all day long that seems to need to be done *then*. It feels like there are larger planning issues here, larger organizational issues that make me nervous.

J: What are you nervous about?

N as Work Ethic Part: I'm worried that all the other things in the business will come up, and I won't do them because I'm loading kilns. Then when I could be doing those business things from 4 to 6, I have agreed to give it over to the Kid and protector. So then all these other business things I haven't done will pile up and affect the kiln loading the next day.

J: So suppose that happens. What's scary about that for you?

N as Work Ethic Part: It feels like I'm the one that's always in charge of figuring out how to get all these things done. There's not enough time, and I'm just overwhelmed. There's no support for figuring out how to do the kiln loading, the jewelry finishing, and the business stuff. That's why I feel I have to work all the time, because nobody helps me figure it out. *They* certainly don't. They just sabotage me, and that makes it worse. It feels like I'm the only responsible one.

As is usually true with protectors, the Work Ethic Part feels overwhelmed partly because it believes it is all alone with this difficult problem. It needs to have the support of Self.

J: So …

N: What's interesting here … I'm going to sit in Self maybe …

J: Good, that's just where I was going to ask you to go.

There has been enough conversation between me and the part. Now Nancy's Self needs to join the discussion because Nancy knows more about this than I do, and ultimately she needs to craft a resolution and work together with her parts to stick to it.

N: I'm in Self, and I can feel that Work Ethic Part starting to get really overwhelmed. It wants to cry. It feels like, "Fine, it's nice to give up a couple hours to play, but they don't understand that there's an enormous amount of other stuff to deal with—phone calls coming in, stuff to be ordered, my worker comes tomorrow, packing and shipping, orders to be pulled. There's just an enormous amount of business stuff." And this Work Ethic Part is the only one that feels responsible and keeps track of it.

J: So it seems like the Work Ethic part needs *you* to support her.

N: Needs Self, yeah.

J: I think you are already doing this, but let's make it explicit. Start by acknowledging to the Work Ethic Part what she's feeling and what she's worried about.

N: As Self, right?

J: Yeah.

N: OK. I understand that you really feel like the buck stops with you. You are totally responsible for the millions of tiny details that go into this business, and you've never really had any support. You just figured out how to do a business all on your own. Nobody taught you anything—about the glass or the business. You invented everything, from buying the packing bags to boxes to shipping to everything. You did figure it all out—this enormous task—and you did a great job.

I understand that you feel responsible for all of it. It's a huge burden. You feel overwhelmed, and you don't understand how you're going to ever get it all done. So even though it's been happening for a good many years now, 4 to 5 years, and you have been very successful, you still feel like you have no help. I understand that you're quite freaked out, anxious, and overwhelmed. I have compassion for how much you've done and how well you've done with no support.

In order for Nancy to really connect with and support the Work Ethic Part, she needs to understand it and convey that understanding and acknowledgment to the part.

J: So switch back to the Work Ethic Part, and see how it's responding to you.

N: So I'm talking back to Self.

J: Mm-hmm.

N as Work Ethic Part: I'm glad you understand how I feel, that I do feel overwhelmed and alone. So I feel a little bit better that you are hearing me, but I don't ever feel that I have any help from you in the midst of the day. It's all well and good to hear me now, but where are you during the day? You're not there! It's just me and these crazy people over here—the Procrastinator and Kid. What are you going to do to help me during the day?

J: So switch back—let's see what your response is.

N as Self: What am I going to do during the day? You're right! Where am I? I don't think I'm there. I don't know why I disappear. I have a feeling I disappear because you guys are so habitual and strong in your positions. I don't know what to say. You're right …

Nancy realizes that she wasn't present in Self during the crucial work times when this polarization came up. This is a main reason it has been so difficult. And it is probably because the parts blended with her and took over.

As to how I might help you … but I don't know if I believe this myself, so this could be interesting. I feel like I could offer a sense of "nowness." I could offer a sense of being in one moment at a time. 'Cause you tend to get all freaked out about the future, with the plans and so much to do. I can see you start thinking into the future and it freaks you out, but I do have the capacity to be in the present.

I don't know if that will help, but I do have the ability to say, "Look, we're just going to do one thing, then we'll see about the next thing." I can offer you breathing, sensing this body, breathing, sensing the present moment, bringing the thoughts back to the present moment, and just doing one thing at a time.

J: Let's see how the Work Ethic Part feels about that.

N as Work Ethic Part: Well, that's a start. I think that would help cut my fear level. 'Cause my fear level really does get revved up by thinking about the future. So yeah, I think I could really use help with coming back to the present. Then maybe I would develop some trust that the present is OK and that we can figure out how the future could be OK. Some kind of mutual trust could come out of that.

The Self has shown the Work Ethic Part what it has to offer, and the part likes that.

I don't know, 'cause I still think I'm responsible for the future ... and planning ...

Even though the Self and the Work Ethic Part have worked out something important, the part says that it is still worried about the future. This tells me that something more is needed, so I bring up an idea.

J: OK, I've got an idea, Nancy.

N: What?

J: Switch back to the Self chair. I want to talk to you in Self for a moment.

N: OK.

J: I heard that the Work Ethic Part is afraid there is just too much work, and there isn't time to give the other parts the playtime and the presence time that they want. I think that has to be addressed. So I'm asking you in Self: Is the Work Ethic Part correct in its fear that there really isn't enough time? Or would there be enough time if you worked the hours you planned, including the playtime?

The Work Ethic Part has a fear that is keeping it from cooperating. It's important to determine whether or not such a fear is realistic. So I ask Nancy to access Self and do some reality testing.

N: I just don't know. Part of me thinks that there would be a lot more time, if it were organized. So I think that I'd like to try this for a week or so—not just for a day—to see if this actually works.

J: Oh, I get it.

N: I think that there's so much sabotaging happening that there's an enormous amount of time being wasted.

J: I get it …

N: But another part of me says, "Well, last week there were two days when I worked nonstop. I didn't do any firing. I did all business stuff, and I never procrastinated at all, and I didn't get any stuff made. So holy cow, I just worked eight hours just doing business stuff. And it was *not* very satisfying; it was sort of horrifying.

J: And you didn't have any fun, either.

N: No, I didn't have any fun. So I mean it wasn't terrible. I was getting stuff done. But I didn't get to do any spontaneous acts. It was a little eye opener, like uh-oh, maybe there isn't as much time as I thought. So I don't know. I actually do not know.

Nancy's thoughtful answer is that she doesn't yet know whether the Work Ethic Part's fears are realistic or not. So she needs to do an experiment to find this out.

J: So it seems that you need to do an experiment, and get an agreement from both sides to actually cooperate, so that there's no sabotage. You set aside time for fun for a whole week, and *see* what actually transpires—whether that gives you enough time for the business or whether it doesn't.

N: Right.

J: It seems to me that you need to promise the parts, from Self, that if it turns out that it *doesn't* give you enough time for the business, that you will do some larger rethinking about your business so that in the end, they can *both* get what they want.

N: Right. That makes sense, yes.

J: So it seems like what you need to ask from each side is: "Are you willing to cooperate for a week in this experiment and see how it goes?" so you will know what to do from there.

N: Yes, 'cause we need to gather data and see what happens in a clean way, instead of just everybody calling each other names.

J: So I'm thinking that you could actually reassure the Work Ethic Part that if she's willing for a week to give the other parts their playtime, then you will evaluate at the end of the week whether it worked or not. You're not asking her to do it permanently and get you in trouble if it doesn't work.

I'm taking an active stance in formulating the experiment and what each part would be agreeing to.

N: So, Work Ethic Part, I need to have an agreement with you that you're willing to calm down your panic and overwhelm for a week while we do this experiment. We will gather data to find out how much work there actually is, and how much time there is, and whether it can all be done. You need to be able to give up a couple, three hours a day to the Kid and the Procrastinator, the putterer, so that they can have some space. And they need to allow you to work when you need to work. Then we'll gather data and we'll find out. And if it doesn't work, we'll look at a whole larger plan after a week's worth of experiment and information gathering. So now I'll talk to the Procrastinator and Kid ...

J: No, wait! See if the Work Ethic Part will agree to that. You can't dictate this. You've got to get her agreement.

Nancy has framed the experiment and what is required from the Work Ethic Part for it to happen, but she can't go ahead without the part actively agreeing to it.

N as Work Ethic Part: Well, I'm willing to give it a try for a week, but I'd like to request some help in laying out the plans—what's going to happen the next day, what you're going to work on. But I've noticed that when we do that, you leave out time for miscellaneous stuff. You just plan the big things, and then all the little things happen and then the big things go out the window. So I need to make sure that you include time for the little things so that I don't feel so overwhelmed when the kiln firings don't happen.

Notice how this dialogue has brought up good ideas about how to better organize the work.

With *that*, I'd be willing to agree to give this plan a week. We work from 9 to 12, have a gap from 12 to 1, make stuff again from 1 to 4, then give the Kid and the Procrastinator from 4 to 6 to play or do whatever they want. Then go ahead and finish stuff in the evening, but hopefully upstairs as opposed to downstairs. So yeah, I'm willing to try this for a week.

J: Good, so go to the other parts now.

N as Procrastinator: So that was interesting. Now I understand the amazing responsibility that Work Ethic Part has. It feels like it's carrying the whole thing. I see that we're just out here in reactive la-la land, doing our own thing and not caring. I realize that I may be reacting to the intensity of the Work Ethic Part's sense of responsibility and overwhelm and fear. So I feel a little softer towards the Work Ethic because it really seems to believe it's carrying the whole deal.

The Procrastinator is really understanding the feelings of the Work Ethic Part. This is important to it cooperating. It realizes that its reactivity is a response to the intense feelings of the Work Ethic Part. This realization is possible because they are really listening to each other and beginning to care about each other.

I could possibly back down a little on my reactivity level. And yeah, I'm willing to give it a week's trial because I like the idea of having blocked-out times when I'm not going to be bugged while I'm playing or protecting the Kid playing. I will actually have *really* free time that I don't have to feel guilty about or feel judged or harassed by the Work Ethic Part. So yeah, that sounds good to me, if we get to go outside from 12 to 1 and from 4 to 6.

I'm even willing to putter with jewelry outside, as long as we get the opportunity to be outside and do fun stuff. I'm willing to even give a little bit there. But the choice needs to be mine. I can't be pushed into it. I want time set aside for whatever I want to do—play and garden and whatever. If I want to work and join in, then that's fine, too, but it's my decision. So I'm willing to try it for a week.

J: What you are being asked to agree to is to *not* sabotage the Work Ethic from 9 to 12 and from 1 to 4 and, I guess, the evening time. *That's* what you're actually being asked to agree to.

The Procrastinator has agreed to the experiment, but it didn't agree to the most crucial part of it, so I bring that up.

N as Procrastinator: Oh well, then that's a different matter. So to *not* sabotage from 9 to 12 … OK. I'm willing to give that a try, but I need to have some way to handle the thoughts that come up, and cool ideas and things. Because I have thoughts popping into my mind all the time, and some of them are good thoughts, and I have this fear that if I don't do them, they're just going to go by the wayside.

I need a way of recording those thoughts that I don't get to act on from 9 to 12 and 1 to 4. So how about if I get to say my ideas into my digital voice recorder, and then if I choose to act on them later, that's fine. That way they're not lost. That's how I figure I can get by with not acting on my thoughts from 9 to 12 and 1 to 4. So with that stipulation, there would be some venting, and I wouldn't just have to shut up. Then I'd be willing to give it a try.

J: Sounds good. Let's see how the Work Ethic Part feels about that.

By going back and forth in hammering out this agreement, the parts are coming up with new, creative ideas about how to make it work. This is a sign that they really are cooperating with each other. This is the deeper goal of polarization work—not just getting a practical resolution to this issue but learning to work together.

N as Work Ethic Part: OK, that sounds workable. I think the digital voice recorder is a good idea because I *know* you have a lot of ideas, and sometimes they're really helpful to the business. You think of stuff that I've forgotten because I'm so overwhelmed. Whenever you have a thought or an idea, please, say it into the digital voice recorder, and then we'll review that later. That will be good because those thoughts won't be lost, and you won't feel so compelled to act on them, but they'll still be there. Now I feel like I do trust you to not sabotage the work.

J: So it sounds like you've got an agreement. Is that right?

N: Yeah, I think that's true. I'm glad that little bit came out about the Procrastinator and the way it distracts. It's because it has these spontaneous ideas that it thinks it has to act on.

J: Yeah, that's a smart thing to have a way to give that part something to do with those ideas.

N: OK, so I think I have a plan, and it feels good that it's going to be for a week.

J: So just check inside and see if all parts are happy with that.

N: Yeah, the Kid we didn't hear from, but the Kid thinks anything new is fun. So it's excited because it's something new and interesting and an experiment, so it's up for it.

J: Let's check one last thing. Is the Kid also willing to not sabotage from 9 to 12 and 1 to 4?

Since the sabotaging has been the problem, we need to make sure that all the parts have agreed to stop.

N: Yeah, let's ask the Kid. Yeah, the Kid's willing to not sabotage. It's willing to go along with it. It likes making jewelry, it likes working, it likes doing stuff. It's fine. This is a fun experiment. It's willing to give it a try. It doesn't feel that reactive. It's more the protector that was reactive.

J: I think that, in addition to having made this agreement, a key to making this work is your being in Self as much as possible during this time.

I am reminding her that just making the agreement isn't enough. She will need to be in Self to support the parts in implementing the agreement and also to monitor the experiment.

N: Right. So it's not just the parts living out this agreement. That would be a little schizophrenic and not too resolving. I want to be there in Self with the parts during their time of day. Does that make sense?

J: Yeah.

N: Self supervising the whole thing and keeping them on track, and gathering the information.

J: OK, is this a place to stop?

N: Yeah, fine.

The one thing we didn't explore in this session was the exile that the Work Ethic Part is protecting. Its fear and overwhelm aren't just due to the situation and the polarization. There must also be an exile underneath. Accessing and healing that exile would also help with resolving this conflict.

Chapter 12

Polarization Role-Playing

T HIS CHAPTER DESCRIBES A POLARIZATION EXERCISE THAT you can use in IFS groups or workshops. I learned it in my IFS Level 1 Training.

One person volunteers to work on a polarization issue. I will call this person the *explorer*. Two other people role-play the explorer's polarized parts, while the explorer participates as Self.

Step 1

The explorer describes each of the polarized parts to the group. This needs to be done in enough detail that group members will be able to role-play them.

Step 2

Two other group members are chosen to role-play these polarized parts. You can ask the explorer to choose a person to play each part, with the understanding that the person chosen can opt out if he or she wants. Alternatively, people in the group can volunteer to play each part. After people are chosen, check to see if they believe they understand their part well enough to play it. If not, ask the explorer to describe the part in more detail until they do.

Step 3

The two role players have a conversation (usually an argument) reflecting the normal way their parts are polarized. During this argument, they stay in the parts' usual extreme roles. The explorer can coach the role players if necessary to make sure they are playing the parts correctly. However, encourage the role players to use their own intuition and experience in acting their roles.

You end this step when the parts' positions have been shown clearly and the polarization conflict has been demonstrated. You will also know to end it if the role players start to repeat themselves.

Step 4

Ask the explorer to explore how he or she has been affected emotionally by observing this argument. It is often quite powerful to see one's psyche demonstrated so vividly. Ask the explorer to share any insights this has brought up.

Ask the explorer if any parts have become activated by watching the argument between the polarized parts. If any exiles have become activated, have the explorer ask them to relax and unblend. Then coach the explorer to provide soothing and nurturing to the exiles from Self.

If any protectors are activated other than the two polarized parts, have the explorer ask them to unblend. Or if they don't right away, do whatever additional work is needed with these protectors for them to unblend.

Step 5

For each polarized part in turn, the explorer should be in Self and working with the part by speaking to the group member who is role-playing the part.

1. Explorer unblends from the polarized part, if necessary.

2. Explorer checks how he or she feels toward the part and unblends from any concerned parts so he or she can be in Self.

3. Explorer gets to know the positive intent of the part and expresses understanding and appreciation for it.

4. Each role player (as part) describes how it feels to get this appreciation.

Step 5

Set up a new dialogue between the role players as the parts, this time reflecting the shifts that are happening in the parts and their relationship as a result of the work that has been done. This dialogue will usually be dramatically different in a very satisfying way. This shift shows the client and the group what is possible in resolving polarization.

Step 6

Ask the explorer to explore how he or she has been affected by observing this transformed dialogue. There is often a feeling of relief and hope.

Step 7

Ask the explorer if he or she has a sense of what exiles are being protected by each polarized part. If the explorer isn't sure, ask the role players if they have a sense of the exiles being protected. Don't try to work with these exiles. That would go beyond the scope of this exercise.

Step 8

Role players formally release their roles and become themselves again. They say: "I am no longer (explorer)'s part. I am (name)." Then each of them shares what it was like to play the role and what it brought up for them.

The explorer reflects on how the entire exercise has affected him or her. Then other group members also share their personal responses to the work.

Chapter 13

Following Up Polarization Work

Working with Polarization in Real Time

When two polarized parts come to an agreement in a session, it isn't the end of the story. The agreement still has to be put into practice. Various contingencies may arise in the moment in the client's life when the solution is put into action. Then more work may be needed.

For example, after Anne heals the exile that the Sheep Part has been protecting, it will probably relax its role to a significant degree. Then the Life Purpose Part will prompt her to work on a project to bring her talents and gifts to the world. This will probably involve her having much more contact with people than she has had in the past. This may trigger the Sheep Part. Even though it may have largely let go of its role, new growth on Anne's part may result in new, possibly threatening interactions with people. If the Sheep Part acts out again, Anne will need to handle it in the moment and possibly do more IFS work in sessions.

After achieving resolution in a session, it is important for the client to practice working with the polarized parts in those moments in his or her life when the polarizing issue comes up. At those times, the client needs to work on having the Self in charge. This means unblending from each part at that time, if necessary.

In addition, the client reminds the parts what happened in the session and asks them to let him or her be in charge now and decide what action to take. This allows the client to make decisions and take action according to what was worked out in the session. These actions should be satisfying for each part and should help the client to be functional and feel good in the situation.

For example, suppose Anne gives a talk or leads a workshop to make her work known in her local area. This might trigger the Sheep Part to make her feel numb and distant from people. At that moment, Anne needs to recognize what is happening and ask the Sheep to step aside and allow her to handle the situation from Self. This would allow her to be open and contactful with the people she meets. She might want to remind the Sheep that the Little Girl is now healed and safe, and she won't be humiliated by the people at her lecture or workshop.

When new or unexpected situations arise, the polarized parts may become triggered anew, and the client may need to engage in further dialogue with one or both parts. During this real-time work, the client may get new insights about the parts that will indicate what to work on in future sessions.

For example, now that the Life Purpose Part is freed, it might start pushing Anne to work overly hard and take on projects that are beyond her current professional experience. Since this part is trying to gain self-worth from this work, it could go overboard and become extreme in this way. This could trigger the Sheep Part to become extreme again, closing her down and pushing her to hide from people.

Then Anne would need to have them dialogue more with each other to work out these new issues. She might also need to work with the exile that the Life Purpose Part is protecting. When that exile is healed, the Life Purpose Part won't be so likely to push her excessively. It can simply be motivated by its true desire to bring her gifts to the world. As a result, the Sheep Part will be less likely to react by trying to close her down.

Similarly, when Nancy is trying out her experiment at work, problems could arise. There might be an extra load of work that comes in one day that tempts the Work Ethic Part to renege on its promise of playtime. This could trigger the Procrastinator to sabotage her work time in retaliation. To avoid this, Nancy would need to be present in Self to remind the parts of their agreement so the Work Ethic Part would honor the playtime that it agreed to.

If this isn't possible on a particular day, any changes to the agreement that day would need to be negotiated with the Procrastinator so that it didn't feel dismissed. If it agrees to a temporary suspension of play, then it won't sabotage her work. This negotiation should be supervised by Nancy in Self.

What If the Client's Behavior Doesn't Change?

What if you seem to have resolved a polarization, but the client's behavior doesn't change? Suppose you come to a resolution of a polarization in the dialogue, or you unburden an exile and its protector seems to relax, but the client continues to engage in the problematic behavior that was the presenting problem. First you should have the client reaccess the part (or parts) that is the source of that behavior and explore why it continues to act the way it does. When you find this out, it will tell you what work you need to do next.

Here are some of the possibilities:

1. You may have only healed one exile. Remember that *each* protector in the polarization is protecting an exile. The protector on the other side of the polarization may still be acting in an extreme way because its exile hasn't yet been healed.

2. The successful work you have done with one exile has now opened up a deeper exile who needs attention.

3. The protector in question might be protecting more than one exile, and you have only healed one of them. For example, suppose Carrie has a polarization between an Overeating Part and a Food Manager. You find the exile that the Overeater has been protecting, a part that was deprived and feels needy, and you heal that exile. However, Carrie's overeating continues. You explore further and discover that she has an Angry Part that has been exiled by the Overeater because of the danger of expressing anger in her family of origin. This anger issue must also be healed before the Overeater will be willing to relax. And Carrie might have even more exiles that this part is protecting, perhaps a starved exile who was bottle-fed.

4. There might be a second part on one side of the polarization. Remember that there are two sides to a polarization, but there can be more than one part on each side. Maybe you have indeed helped to transform one polarized part or even both of them, but there might be two

parts on one side of the polarization, and you haven't identified the second one. One of them has shifted, but the other hasn't. You will need to discover that other part and work with it.

For example, suppose Don has a polarization between a Taskmaster Part that pushes him to work very hard and a Procrastinator that avoids essential tasks because it is afraid of failing. You work successfully with those two, but Don continues to avoid important work. Then you discover that Don also has a Rebel Part that is defying the Taskmaster because it doesn't want to be dominated by that part (and Don had a dominating father). The Rebel is obviously on the same side of the polarization as the Procrastinator. You must help Don work with the Rebel and get its cooperation in order to successfully resolve the issue.

5. Perhaps the original polarization has indeed been resolved, but some other part feels threatened by that. This part could undermine the resolution. You will need to find this part and work with it so it becomes comfortable with the changes that ensue from resolving the polarization. For example, suppose Don resolves his procrastination issues and starts accomplishing a great deal and becoming quite successful. This might trigger a part that is afraid of success. This part will try to undermine the previous unburdenings and polarization solutions in order to keep Don from being successful. You must uncover this part and help it unburden its fear.

The human psyche can be very complex. Don't assume that just because you have followed the IFS procedure and unburdened and transformed parts, the client's behavior will change right away. One piece of behavior can have multiple determinants—that is, multiple parts. When the external change that the client seeks is not happening, explore inside until you discover why. Then work on the parts you discover until all of them have been healed and transformed and the polarization has been resolved.

Chapter 14

Polarization in Larger Systems

POLARIZATION DOESN'T JUST HAPPEN INTERNALLY. Polarizations also exist between people in larger systems, such as couples, families, and organizations. Most common is polarization between two people, especially two people in a close relationship, such as a marriage. It is common for a couple to become polarized around issues they face in their lives. For example, they might polarize around the best way to handle a child-rearing situation. This can lead to endless fights.

Because of the polarization dynamics between marriage partners, they will each tend to become extreme in order to advocate for their position, just as parts do. They may each forget about the parts of them that might agree with their partner because that would soften their stance, and they are afraid of giving in. However, this strategy results in the two battling rather than understanding each other.

For example, Ed and Martha disagree about how strict to be about their daughter Caroline's bedtime. Martha is willing to be loose about it at times, while Ed wants to keep it consistent every night. He becomes even more rigid than he really feels in order to counter what he perceives as Martha's tendency to indulge Caroline. Martha advocates for more flexibility than she really believes is good in order to fight against Ed's rigidity.

There are also polarizations between groups such as organizations, communities, political parties, or countries. Right now, there is extreme polarization in our government between the left and right. Many polarizations form around specific hot-button issues, such as abortion. These polarizations are similar in dynamics to polarizations between parts. Both people or sides justify their extreme behavior and attitude as necessary to fight against the extremes of the other side and the dangers they fear would occur if the other side gained power.

Many of us participate in these larger group polarizations by completely identifying with one side and vilifying the other side. However, we often have a part that agrees to some extent with the other side, even if this part is not prominent in our consciousness. When we get rigidly polarized around an issue, we tend to exile any parts of us that might have some understanding of or agreement with the other side.

For example, suppose that you believe in a woman's right to choose abortion. There might also be a part of you that has misgiving about taking the life of a fetus. However, to allow this part room in your psyche might feel as if it would threaten your ability to advocate for abortion rights. So you might exile this part and become a strident advocate for abortion. However, in the long run, this will probably backfire because it will make it virtually impossible for you to dialogue successfully with someone who is against abortion. And dialogue is really the best way to resolve these issues, both internally in your psyche and externally in the world.

So our internal polarizations are affected by these larger polarizations in the world. If you identify the polarizations inside you that are influenced in this way, and work on resolving them, then you are more equipped to participate in healing the splits in our society and culture.

Projecting Internal Polarizations onto External Ones

Suppose you have an internal polarization, perhaps between a part that wants to eat freely and a part that wants to lose weight. If another person takes one side of this polarization, such as pushing you to lose weight, this is likely to bring out the polarized part in you, the part that wants to enjoy food. If this person pushes you a lot about dieting, you may lose sight of your internal polarization and become completely blended with only one side—in this case, the side that wants to eat freely. The dieter part of you gets exiled because its position has been taken up by the other person, who is perceived as oppressive and harmful. Your internal polarization has become projected onto the external relationship.

This kind of polarization is common with couples, where one person always advocates for one side of a polarization, such as having fun, and the other person always takes the opposite stance, such as being responsible. The partners lose track of the fact that each person has internal parts on both sides of the polarization, and this makes it hard for them to dialogue constructively about the issue.

The same kind of thing can happen when *you* are relating to someone who is polarized. If you are close to someone who has an internal polarization and you take a strong stance for one side, you will probably hear only from the opposed part of that person and never realize that they have a side that agrees with you. And worse, the other person may not realize it, either.

Many a parent has stepped into this trap with a child or teenager. You take the side of responsibility, and he or she takes the side of freedom, losing touch with his or her responsible side. While the teenager may have a polarization inside about being a responsible person versus having fun all the time, if you take the responsible side, the teen may come down entirely on the fun side in order to fight against you. You are much more likely to be effective in dialoguing with someone if you can empathize with both sides of his or her polarization. Then the other person is more likely to trust you and be open to your perspective. And he or she is more likely to be aware of a part that agrees with you.

Appendix A

Polarization Help Sheet

THIS HELP SHEET CAN BE USED AS A REFERENCE WHEN YOU are working with a polarization. It uses the seven steps that I have elaborated to teach the method developed by Richard Schwartz.

1. Recognize and identify the polarized parts.

2. Facilitate the client in unblending from each part in order to access Self.

    a. Have the client hold each part in consciousness at the same time.

    b. Ask each part to step aside so the client can get to know the other part.

    c. Have the client reassure each part that he or she will get to know it, too, and won't let the other part take over.

3. Facilitate the client in getting to know each part's role, positive intent, and conflict with the other part.

    a. Unblend from any concerned parts.

    b. Find out what the part is trying to do for the client.

    c. Find out how the part feels toward the polarized part and how it counters it.

    d. Develop a trusting relationship between the client's Self and each part.

4. Decide whether to work with an exile or engage in a depolarization dialogue.

5. Have the client get permission from each part to have a depolarization dialogue with the other part under the guidance of Self.

    a. Reassure each part that Self won't allow the other part to take over or attack.

6. Facilitate the beginning of the depolarization dialogue.

    a. Decide whether to do it internally or externally.

    b. Have each part state its position and respond to the other part.

    c. Continue the process until the positions and conflict are clear.

7. Facilitate true dialogue and resolution.

    a. Each part reveals the exile it is protecting.

    b. Each part listens to the other's concerns and fears, and responds accordingly.

    c. Either a part, the Self, or the therapist suggests a resolution.

    d. Each part considers the potential resolution and brings up concerns and suggestions for improving it.

e. The parts negotiate with each other and Self in order to come to a resolution they can both agree to.

Appendix B

Glossary

Accessing a Part Tuning in to a part experientially, through an image, an emotion, a body sensation, or internal dialogue

Blending The situation in which a part has taken over the client's consciousness so that he or she feels its feelings, believes its attitudes are true, and acts according to its impulses

Burden A painful emotion or negative belief about oneself or the world that a part has taken on as a result of a past harmful situation or relationship, usually from childhood

Concerned Part A part that feels judgmental or angry toward the target part. When a client is blended with a concerned part, he or she isn't in Self.

Depolarization Dialogue An exchange in which two or more parts have a conversation with each other in order to resolve their polarization

Dialogue A conversation between two parts (or people) in which each is genuinely trying to hear the other's perspective and cooperate

Direct Access   A form of IFS therapy in which the therapist speaks directly to a part, and the client is blended with the part and responds to the therapist *as* the part. This also can involve two parts speaking to each other as the client blends first with one and then the other.

Disowned Exile   An exile that is being kept out of consciousness, not because it is in pain, but because it was unacceptable in the milieu in which the person grew up

Dissociative Firefighter   A firefighter that protects an exile by using dissociation

Exile   A young child part that is carrying pain from the past

External Dialogue   A depolarization dialogue that is done using direct access, in which the client sits in a different chair for each part and speaks as the part

Extreme Role   A role that is dysfunctional or problematic because the part carries a burden from the past or because a protector is trying to protect an exile

Firefighter   A type of protector that reacts impulsively in the moment when the pain of an exile is arising in order to numb the pain or distract the client from it

Healthy Role   A role that is the natural function of a part when it has no burdens

Internal Dialogue   A form of depolarization dialogue that happens entirely internal to the client. The parts speak to each other in an internal space, and the client reports what they say to the therapist.

Manager   A type of protector that proactively tries to arrange a person's life and psyche so that the pain of exiles never rises to consciousness

One-Sided Polarization   A situation in which one part is fighting against another part, but the second part is not fighting back

Part   A subpersonality, which has its own feelings, perceptions, beliefs, motivations, and memories

Polarization   A dynamic in which two or more parts are in conflict about how a person feels or behaves in a particular situation

Positive Intent   The underlying helpful or protective goal that motivates a part to perform its role, even if the effect of the role is negative

Protector   A part that tries to block off pain that is arising or to protect the person from hurtful incidents or distressing relationships

Role   The job that a part performs to help a client. It may be primarily internal, or it may involve the way the part interacts with people and acts in the world.

Self   The core aspect of a person that is his or her true self or spiritual center. The Self is relaxed, open, and accepting of the person and others. It is curious, compassionate, calm, and interested in connecting with other people and with the person's parts.

Target Part   The part one is focusing on at the moment

Trailhead   A psychological issue involving one or more parts that can lead to healing if followed.

Unblending   Separating from a part that is blended with a person, so that he or she can be in Self

Unburdening   The step in the IFS process in which the Self helps an exile to release its burdens through an internal ritual

Witnessing   The step in the IFS process in which the Self witnesses the childhood origin of a part's burdens

Appendix C

IFS Resources

IFS Therapists

If you want to find an IFS therapist to work with, consult the website of the Center for Self Leadership, the official IFS organization, at www.selfleadership.org. This listing of therapists who have completed Level 1 of the IFS professional training can be searched by geographical location. Some of these therapists offer IFS sessions by telephone.

IFS Professional Training and Consultation

The Center for Self Leadership conducts training programs in IFS for therapists and others in the helping professions, which I highly recommend. There are three levels of training, which can be taken one at a time. Level 1 consists of six three-day weekends. These training programs are held in many cities in the U.S. and in Europe. The trainers are excellent, and the curriculum is well designed. These are experiential trainings, so you learn about IFS by working with your own parts and practicing doing sessions with others in the training. The training group emphasizes building community, which fosters personal and professional connection. See the CSL website, www.

selfleadership.org, for details about training locations and schedules.

I lead IFS consultation groups over the telephone, and I offer a variety of training courses and workshops, many by telephone. These include a course on polarization. See my IFS website, www.personal-growth-programs.com, for a complete list of offerings.

IFS Classes and Groups

I teach classes for the general public in which people learn to use IFS for self-help and peer counseling. The classes can be taken by telephone or in person in the San Francisco Bay Area. Each class is either a six-week course or a weekend workshop. Some of the classes are taught by my wife, Bonnie Weiss, and other highly skilled IFS therapists and teachers. We also offer IFS classes and workshops on polarization, procrastination, eating issues, intimacy, communication, and other topics.

I also offer ongoing IFS therapy groups in person and ongoing IFS classes over the telephone. See www.personal-growth-programs.com for more information and a schedule of classes and groups.

IFS Books

Introduction to the Internal Family System Model, by Richard Schwartz. A basic introduction to parts and IFS for clients and potential clients.

Internal Family Systems Therapy, by Richard Schwartz. The primary professional book on IFS and a must-read for therapists.

The Mosaic Mind, by Richard Schwartz and Regina Goulding. A professional book on using IFS with trauma, especially sexual abuse.

You Are the One You've Been Waiting For, by Richard Schwartz. A popular book providing an IFS perspective on intimate relationships.

Self-Therapy: A Step-by-Step Guide to Creating Wholeness and Healing Your Inner Child Using IFS, by Jay Earley. Shows how to do IFS sessions on your own or with a partner. Also a manual of the IFS method that can be used by therapists.

Self-Therapy for Your Inner Critic, by Jay Earley and Bonnie Weiss. Shows how to use IFS to work with inner critic parts.

Illustrated Workbook for Self-Therapy for Your Inner Critic, by Bonnie Weiss. A graphic support containing illustrations from the book in large format and grouped for easy understanding.

Parts Work, by Tom Holmes. A short, richly illustrated introduction to IFS for the general public.

Bring Yourself to Love, by Mona Barbera. A book for the general public on using IFS to work through difficulties in love relationships.

IFS Articles and Recordings

The Center for Self-Leadership website, www.selfleadership.org, contains professional articles by Richard Schwartz on IFS. He has produced a number of excellent videos of IFS sessions he has conducted, which can be purchased from the website. The website also has audio recordings of presentations from past IFS conferences.

IFS Conferences and Workshops

The annual IFS conference is an excellent opportunity to delve more deeply into the Model and network with other professionals. Richard Schwartz leads week-long personal growth workshops open to the public at various growth centers in the U.S. and Mexico. Other professional workshops and presentations on IFS are also offered by Schwartz as well as other senior IFS trainers. See www.selfleadership.org for details.

My Websites and Applications

My IFS website, www.personal-growth-programs.com, contains popular and professional articles on IFS and its application to various psychological issues, and more are being added all the time. You can also join the email list to receive future articles and notification of upcoming classes and groups.

My personal website, www.jayearley.com, contains more of my writings and information about my practice, including my therapy groups.

Another website, www.psychemaps.com, contains a free Inner Critic Questionnaire and Profiling Program for understanding your Inner Critic and developing an Inner Champion to deal with it.

I am developing a web application for doing self-therapy online using IFS. It should be available by the fall of 2012.

Appendix D

Managers and Firefighters

E VEN THOUGH *RESOLVING INNER CONFLICT* IS PRIMARILY about polarization, I include this appendix on managers and firefighters for two reasons. One is that these two types of protectors are frequently polarized, so understanding them is helpful. Second, this book is a follow-up to my previous book *Self-Therapy,* which did not explain this distinction.

Managers and *firefighters* are the two types of IFS protectors. Managers try to arrange a person's life and psyche so that the pain of exiles never arises. For example, Bill has a manager that tries to keep him from reaching out to women for fear that he will be rejected.

Firefighters react impulsively when an exile has been triggered. They attempt to squash the exile's pain or distract the client from it. When a firefighter is triggered, a client may not be aware of the pain starting to arise. He or she may only experience the firefighter reaction. For example, when Bill calmed his manager enough to call Sandra for a date, it was clear from her response that she didn't want to go out with him. This started to bring up the pain of an exile who felt rejected, but Bill didn't realize this because he immediately started drinking. His alcohol firefighter came in so fast that he didn't even feel the exile's pain. The drinking numbed him.

Managers are *proactive,* and firefighters are *reactive.* Managers act with foresight to stave off pain, for example, by trying to keep Bill away from attractive women. Firefighters react impulsively to keep pain from arising into consciousness, often with numbing or addictive activities. If you think of managers as adults and exiles as children in one's internal family, firefighters are teenagers who react impulsively to put out the fire of an exile's pain.

Firefighters

Managers are much more common than firefighters for most people, and they are the parts we usually think of when we refer to protectors. The rest of this chapter will focus on the distinctive characteristics of firefighters and how to work with them.

Firefighters have the job of putting out the fire of the pain that erupts from an exile. Real-life firefighters will charge into a dangerous situation to extinguish a fire, sometimes without worrying about the consequences to their own welfare. Think of the firefighters who rushed into the skyscrapers during 9/11 without concern for their own lives. Our internal firefighters are similar in their disregard for our well-being. They will do anything to numb us or distract us from pain that is coming up. They fear that the pain will be overwhelming, so they ignore the possible destructive consequences of their actions. Anything to get away from the pain!

The following are activities that are often initiated by firefighters: abusing drugs or alcohol, sexual acting out, overeating, compulsive shopping, gambling, and other addictions. Firefighters can also produce rage, dissociation, falling asleep, running away, shutting down, or thrill-seeking activities. In addition, more ordinary actions can be used by firefighters as distractions, for example, reading, watching TV, and headaches.

The activities listed above don't always come from firefighters—and almost any activity or feeling state *can* come from a firefighter. The crucial question is whether it is an ongoing, proactive activity (manager) or whether it is an impulsive reaction to exile pain (firefighter).

Working with Firefighters

Firefighters are often less verbal than managers, which means they may not communicate in words, or it may be hard to get them to respond with internal dialogue. They may also be harder to negotiate with; they just want to perform their roles. This is especially true of dissociative firefighters, which cause a client to fog out, space out, or fall asleep, for example. In fact, when a client dissociates, it can be difficult to believe that this is coming from a part, since it seems like such an automatic bodily reaction. When you first try to work with a dissociative firefighter by having the client ask it a question, he or she may get no verbal response from the part.

However, don't give up. If you spend some time helping the client to access and get to know a dissociative firefighter, it will usually come around and respond and eventually engage in a dialogue.

You may have to spend more time helping a client to just *be with* a firefighter rather than asking it too many questions. Doing this helps in gaining its trust. Don't push to get the firefighter to respond to your client if it is resistant. Just encourage the client to hang out with it, the way you would patiently be with a wild animal that was afraid of humans. The firefighter will slowly begin to trust the client (and you) enough to reveal itself.

Accessing Self

It can be difficult for clients to truly be in Self with respect to firefighters because they are often destructive and hard to communicate with. This makes it difficult to believe that they have a positive intent—that they are trying to protect and help the client. Remember that firefighters are doing what they think is crucial to protect a client from intolerable pain.

To work with a client's firefighter, first you must make sure that *you* are in Self with respect to the firefighter. You must be truly interested in getting to know the part from its own perspective rather than just trying to get past it to the exile underneath. Remember that the firefighter is really trying to help the client, even though that may be difficult to imagine, given how much havoc it is causing. If you have parts that dislike a firefighter or parts that want to brush it aside, ask them to relax so you can really welcome the firefighter and get to know it.

Once you are in Self, help the client to get in Self, too. This may require some education about firefighters—explaining to the client that they really are parts, not just bodily reactions, and that they are actually trying to protect the client from pain that is arising.

You will often need to work with the parts of the client that hate the firefighter and want to get rid of it. I call these "concerned parts"[13] because they have concerns about the firefighter. Make sure to validate concerned parts before asking them to step aside. It is completely understandable that a client would have parts that feel negatively toward a firefighter, given how destructive most firefighters are. So acknowledge these parts' concerns, and then have the client ask them to step aside so he or she can get to know the firefighter from an open place. This allows the client to discover the positive intent of the firefighter and develop a trusting relationship with it, which is an important step in the overall therapeutic process.

Remember that there is a lot to be gained by getting to know troublesome firefighters. They often engage in behaviors that cause serious consequences in our clients' lives, and our clients needs to be connected to them to help them change. Don't just try to get past them. Genuinely take some time to focus on a firefighter and understand it, and especially to help the client develop a trusting relationship with it. This work is just as important as witnessing and healing an exile.

Firefighters especially respond to hope. Once you understand why a firefighter performs its role, it can be helpful to ask a question about a possible new role for the part. Have the client ask, "If we could heal the exile you are protecting, would you still need to perform your role?" "If you didn't have to do this job, what would you prefer to do?" This often gives the firefighter hope that it can let go of a role it feels stuck in. And it provides an inducement for the firefighter to grant permission for you to work with the exile it is protecting.

-----

13. For a detailed explanation of unblending from concerned parts, see chapter 6 of *Self-Therapy*.

Made in the USA
Coppell, TX
04 January 2020